Doctor Steel

Celebrating 35 Years of
Penguin Random House India

'Jamshed Irani and I have been associated with Tata Steel for over thirty-four years. The most significant contribution we have made in Tata Steel has been the modernization of the steel plant at Jamshedpur, which has enabled the company to upgrade its capability and to define a leadership role in the Indian steel industry. Jamshed led the company as its managing director and established a close relationship with the workforce and the trade union, while continuing to upgrade the quality of life in the town of Jamshedpur, converting the town and its facilities from an ageing township into a modern township with modern facilities and comforts'—Ratan N. Tata, chairman, Tata Trusts

'Doc was the embodiment of the Tata ethos. He was innovative and progressive, a leader who brought integrity and caring to the workplace, a devoted citizen of a country he worked daily to modernize and improve. His book is testament to this'—Jamshyd Godrej, chairman and managing director, Godrej & Boyce

'This is a book full of fascinating stories narrated by an iconic Tata leader whom I greatly admired and respected. Dr J.J. Irani's recollections are punctuated with memorable anecdotes and thoughtful reflections. In these pages, you will discover a remarkable man who led Tata Steel with firm resolve, integrity, conviction, warmth and humanity. His life holds invaluable lessons for all of us'—Harish Bhat, brand custodian, Tata Sons, and bestselling author of #Tata Stories and Office Secrets

'J.J. Irani had the kind of stuff in him that leaders are made of. One does not readily come across a corporate leader of his stature. The purpose of telling this story is not merely to revere the dead but to inspire the living—the bearers of his legacy. Dr Irani is not with us, yet he lives on in our memory'—A.M. Misra, former chairman, Tata Sponge Iron, and former vice president, Tata Steel

'In Jamshed Irani's death, Tata has lost a blue-blooded son, and I have lost a close friend and mentor. I wanted him to write a book for the longest time, and the resulting anecdotes are incredibly rich'—R. Gopalakrishnan, former director, Tata Sons

Doctor Steel

My Life and Times with THE TATAS

J.J. IRANI

PENGUIN
BUSINESS

An imprint of Penguin Random House

PENGUIN BUSINESS

USA | Canada | UK | Ireland | Australia
New Zealand | India | South Africa | China | Singapore

Penguin Business is part of the Penguin Random House group of companies
whose addresses can be found at global.penguinrandomhouse.com

Published by Penguin Random House India Pvt. Ltd
4th Floor, Capital Tower 1, MG Road,
Gurugram 122 002, Haryana, India

First published in Penguin Business by Penguin Random House India 2023

ISBN 9780143464440

Typeset in Sabon by Manipal Technologies Limited, Manipal
Printed at Thomson Press India Ltd, New Delhi

www.penguin.co.in

Contents

Part III: Alliances, Encounters and Reflections

Foreword

I joined Tata Steel in 1988 and have had a ringside view of the impact Dr Irani had on Tata Steel during the epochal decade of the 1990s. He had just taken over after a fairly bitter succession battle that had divided the company and after the opening up of the Indian economy in 1991, when many people were questioning whether Tata Steel would survive.

He led from the front with great credibility and took a lot of tough calls at the cost of personal popularity, because it was the right thing to do for the company. He not only transformed Tata Steel physically but also culturally. He brought in the total quality management (TQM) culture and a culture of continuous improvement, which differentiate us even today. He invested in technology, improved productivity, made us a more customer-focused organization, and by the time he had finished he had made us the lowest-cost producer of steel in the world. We were the first company in the Tata Group to win the coveted JRD QV award for excellence.

While it is well known that, along with the union leadership, he drove the transformation of the unionized workforce, what is less well known is that we restructured the executive ranks of the organization dramatically a year before his tenure was to end.

He was very clear that it was a tough call that he himself had to take and not leave for his successor. Many in the leadership team of Tata Steel today, including me, were identified to be among the top 110 leaders of Tata Steel then, even though we were in our mid-thirties at that time. So in many ways, his decisions and actions during his tenure not only made Tata Steel a strong company then but also ensured that we stayed a strong and resilient enterprise many decades later.

As Dr Irani settled in Jamshedpur after his retirement, I had the privilege of spending time with him often, and it was always a pleasure to hear his thoughts and views. He had strong views but was always open to a debate or discussion, and was willing to change his views if he was convinced of the same. He always had Tata Steel's best interests in his mind, and hence always had suggestions on what could be done better and what was good for the company. Even in his last few days at the hospital, he had feedback for me, and that exemplified his passion for excellence and for the company. He has shaped me as a person and a professional in more ways than he may have realized.

I must also acknowledge the role of Daisy Irani and the way she complemented and supplemented him. She went out of her way to make everyone feel comfortable, even if they were intimidated by Dr Irani.

Of the children, I knew Zubin the best, and it is very clear that Dr Irani was a great father, as much as he was a great leader for Tata Steel.

On a personal note, I had the privilege of sharing my birthday with Dr Irani, and hence was always invited by Dr Irani and Daisy Irani to spend the evening at their home if I was in Jamshedpur.

Dr Irani was truly the right person to lead Tata Steel in the 1990s and set up a strong foundation on which the rest of us could build a resilient organization. His imprint on Tata Steel will be felt for many decades to come, and many of us are privileged to have been part of the organization when he transformed it. He is respected as an industry leader way beyond Tata Steel.

I must thank N.K. Sharan for spending the time that he did to capture Dr Irani's thoughts and views, and share them with us. Most of us know about Dr Irani's professional life far more than his personal life, and so it is fascinating to see how his experiences shaped him.

Thank you, Dr Irani, for leading the way.

T.V. Narendran
CEO and managing director, Tata Steel

Introduction

Writing the introduction to Dr Jamshed Irani's memoir has been the most exciting task and a profound honour for me. The various compilations and memories recorded in this book have also been a source of joy. The book you hold in your hands was not initially thought of as a memoir. The story goes like this.

I joined Tata Steel in 1986, as a graduate engineer, immediately after passing out from my engineering college and have worked only in the Tata Group. I had a long and close relationship with Dr Irani. Sometime during 2019, I started nudging him to record for me a few anecdotes from his professional career, which I could use during my corporate training sessions. (My current job at the Tata Business Excellence Group involves a lot of interaction with all sets of corporate professionals, from CEOs to mid-level managers.) I requested Dr Irani to share his experiences with me, particularly the memories of his personal interactions with J.R.D. Tata, and some learning points from his long and extremely successful professional career. Dr Irani accepted the idea, and he recorded one or two small sessions.

As we worked, Dr Irani took great care to go through the transcripts of the recordings with his detail-oriented eyes, marking corrections with a red pen and again going through the revised transcripts. Only when he was satisfied with the transcripts would he allow me to use them for any purpose. This cycle of recording, transcribing, correcting and redoing the same again and again could be a very boring exercise, but Dr Irani started enjoying it. In between, he would reminisce about how Mr Gopalakrishnan (R. Gopalakrishnan, lovingly called RG, was Dr Irani's close colleague at Tata Sons) used to nudge him all the time to author a book. Dr Irani's reply would always be the same, 'Gopal, you are good at writing, I am not.' But when he saw the physical printouts of his transcripts and began a deeper engagement with them, his resistance to the idea of writing a book started to melt. By this time, many of his recordings and transcripts had started becoming potential material for a memoir. It was during the Covid outbreak in 2020, when our frequency of meetings had gone up—as both of us were travelling less—that I proposed to Dr Irani that we should orient our objective to publish a memoir. This idea also got support by Daisy Irani, his life partner for more than fifty years, and his son, Zubin Irani.

As we prepared for publication, Dr Irani enlisted the support of Harish Bhat, brand custodian of Tata Group and an accomplished author. While we processed the content, we required someone to provide a coherent framework for the assorted compilations and to facilitate connections with a suitable publisher. Harish played a pivotal role in shaping the book's preliminary structure, and he also introduced us to Milee Ashwarya, publisher at Penguin Random House India. The invaluable contributions of both Harish and Milee were indispensable in the successful publication of this book.

The result is here in front of you.

* * *

Before we proceed any further, it is important for the reader to understand the context of Tata Steel at the time Dr Irani began his journey, i.e., in the early 1990s.

In the late 1980s and early 1990s, Tata Steel was a rusting, smoking and antiquated steel plant. Its facilities were ancient. During our early years in Tata Steel (1986–92)—I still remember very clearly—it was invariably compared with the Steel Authority of India (SAIL). Even if Tata Steel's performance had been inefficient, it was considered a good performance if it was better than that of SAIL. Tata Steel had a poor standard on the people-productivity front and was labelled as one of the most expensive steel producers in the world. McKinsey at one point called it an inefficient operator in a sunset industry. During 1993–94, it had around 78,000 people producing 2.45 million tonnes of crude steel per year. (Currently, Tata Steel India produces around 20 million tonnes of crude steel with around 32,000 people.) Some of the Japanese and European steel companies had 10X productivity.

Tata Steel had a very strong paternalistic culture. Several hundreds of employees were second- or third-generation employees. The HR policy used to be that if you had worked in the company for twenty-five years, you were guaranteed that your son or daughter could also work there. So, in a way, it was a kind of beyond-life employment. Cost was not a worry. Government regulators would ensure that Tata Steel sold what it produced. Producing more than the government-mandated numbers was penalized. In fact, it is well documented that Tata Steel did not know for many years how many people were on its payrolls—such was the sense of complacency in terms of cost and productivity.

Dr Irani reminisces in this memoir, 'The government told us what to make, how much to make, whom to sell to and how much to charge. What we paid as salaries was recompensed to us by the government through the steel price. If someone in the government asked for a job for a niece or nephew, Tata Steel would more often than not say okay.' As a result, he says, 'we had no incentive to modernize.'

Building and Transforming Tata Steel into a World-Class Enterprise

Dr Irani's commitment to Tata Steel and Tata Group was legendary. He joined Tata Steel in January 1968, as assistant to the director of R&D, and superannuated in July 2001, as managing director, a long and fulfilling thirty-three years at the organization. In this time, he occupied the position of chief metallurgist (1971), general manager operations (1978), president (1985) and joint managing director (1988). He became managing director in 1992, a position he held for nine years, till 2001. Post 2001 he became director of Tata Sons and chairman of TQMS (Tata Quality Management Services, now called Tata Business Excellence Group). He hung up his boots in 2011.

Dr Irani reinvented and transformed Tata Steel from an old-fashioned and outdated entity to one of the most modern and lowest-cost producers of steel in the world. I have also been a part of that journey with these change-enabling institutions (Total Quality Management [TQM] and Tata Business Excellence Group [TBExG]). Like many others, I have experienced every bit of the excitement of these transformations. Having visited Japan and closely observed Japanese companies several times, Dr Irani was inspired by their TQM philosophy. He had found it to be an answer to the massive cultural and attitudinal change which he wanted to bring at Tata Steel. In 1990, he formed a small group in his office called the Total Quality Implementation (TQI) group, which drafted the first quality policy of Tata Steel.

One of my earliest interactions with Dr Irani was in 1992. I was attending a newly formed platform of a Quality Coordinators meet, organized by the TQI group to cascade the new quality policy and philosophy to every Tata Steel department. I saw Dr Irani talking passionately about the new vision embedded in the quality policy of Tata Steel. He spoke about Tata Steel's aspirations to become a supplier of world-class goods and services by anticipating and exceeding the expectations of its customers. Tata Steel had never considered such aspirational customer service so far. This was a watershed moment for me, which not only gave me the clarity of transformation which Dr Irani was passionately seeking from all of us but also served as a tremendous source of inspiration for me to become a part of this movement. Post the formal meeting, for the first time, I met him on the sidelines, like many others. I don't think he would have registered my name, but I was very clear that I had to work with him on this journey.

Later, I joined the TQM department (TQI was changed to TQM), and I feel honoured to have been interviewed by him for my entry into that august corporate group. Dr Irani was one of the pioneers of the TQM movement in the country and helped build a strong foundation on which Tata Steel grew in the subsequent decades. He led with courage and conviction, and was definitely a role model and mentor for many in Tata Steel.

As president and then joint managing director, Dr Irani was very clear that Tata Steel needed to modernize its plants, equipment and technology, and for that it needed a huge capital. He knew that Japanese companies, the gold standard in steel, were operating at a higher debt–equity ratio, and perhaps the same thing had to be done in India to raise capital. He also understood that if one raised capital through debt, the execution of the project became extremely critical to service the debt. He had a clear-cut focus on project execution. Dr Irani's era was no doubt one of the best eras of on-time and efficient project execution. He provided a strong and visionary leadership not only to Tata Steel but to the entire Indian industry.

Post 1992, the forces of liberalization, privatization and globalization demanded an old-fashioned and outdated elephant to dance on its feet. Earlier, steel prices had been controlled by the government, so naturally, steel companies had made limited money. Capital for investment expenditure was scarce. Despite these constraints, Dr Irani could convince the Tata Steel board and got the required capital for various modernization plans. Post 1990, Tata Steel began to modernize its facilities and plants. Tata Steel had never seen such frenetic execution of brown-field capex projects. ('Brown field' means that the land was already in use; the old project had to be dismantled first to facilitate the execution of a new one. Brown-field are more complex than green-field projects.) Despite the lack of experience, most of these capex projects were successfully executed on time and without any major cost overrun. The result of all these efforts was that when Dr Irani superannuated as managing director of Tata Steel in 2001, the only old relic that remained at the Jamshedpur plant was its boundary wall, as the saying goes. Everything inside had been modernized, including the mindset of people working there.

By 2003, Tata Steel had become not only the lowest-cost producer of steel in the world, but also the most modern and efficient steel plant worldwide. Tata Steel's performance between 1990 and 2001 was marked by a focus on modernization, expansion, diversification and efficiency improvements, which helped to position it as the leading player in the Indian steel industry.

In any large-scale transformation, it is relatively easier to change the hardware (the plants, equipment and technology) than changing the software (people's mindset and processes). Dr Irani understood this challenge well. Many Tata Steel workers at the time were not very educated. The middle management was committed but needed a complete overhaul of their mindset. The top management also needed to quickly align itself to Dr Irani's vision and speed of transformation. Dr Irani called this initiative the 'modernization of minds'; there were also other programmes, centred on cost benchmarking and reduction, TQM, TBEM (Tata Business Excellence Model), etc. Through such focused initiatives, Dr Irani could build a strong culture of quality, customer orientation and continuous improvement. Tata Steel's competitive advantage, even today, in my view, lies significantly on this solid foundation of unique continuous improvement and innovation culture.

Dr Irani's ability to simultaneously focus on the 'yin' (modernization and technology) and 'yang' (people and processes) of business made Tata Steel's transformation a very comprehensive and holistic exercise.

His visit to Japanese companies had given him a clear sense of the role of employee participation in any transformation exercise. Thousands of team-based improvement projects (e.g., Quality Circles, Quality Improvement Projects, Value Engineering Projects) were taken up as part of TQM/TBEM initiatives to engage 100 per cent of the employees. Strategic initiatives included the reduction of workforce through the Early Separation scheme, the restructuring of marketing and sales processes, SAP (a software system for the management of business processes), execution in supply chain, focused cost reduction, etc. All these were executed with equal force.

Dr Irani loved the workers and was always concerned about their welfare. He would spend disproportionate amounts of time attending Join Development Council (JDC) meetings. (The JDC was a platform for the union and management.) When it came to recognizing good workers, be it through 'Quality Circles' or the suggestions box or the JDC, Dr Irani did the honours himself and never delegated the job to any of his executives. It was his visible commitment to the Total Quality movement. His relationship with the union was based on credibility and trust, as he never hesitated in speaking the truth.

Relationships with Key External Stakeholders

In the late 1990s, Dr Irani had realized that in order to grow, Tata Steel had to go beyond Jamshedpur. Dr Irani's relationship with Lalu Prasad Yadav, the then chief minister of Bihar, was really good. He built similarly cordial relationships with Biju Patnaik and J.B. Patnaik, the chief ministers of Odisha, even though both were political opponents of each other.

During his tenure as the president of the Confederation of Indian Industry (CII), Dr Irani did quite a lot of work to strengthen the Indo–British partnership. He built a personal rapport with Queen Elizabeth II and John Major, the then prime minister of the UK. Subsequently, he got recognition from the British government in the form of an honorary knighthood (KBE) for his work. Even at the Government of India level, Dr Irani was a well-known and respected figure, on good terms with everyone from the prime minister to important bureaucrats.

Doing Fair and Honest Business

During my conversations with Dr Irani, he mentioned various instances and challenges he faced while dealing with a section of politicians and bureaucrats. He added that what helped him every time was his principled stand, of doing fair and honest business. Dr Irani, in his own words, 'vociferously stood for the Tata way' when it came to addressing the challenges in dealing with politicians and bureaucrats. 'Tatas should not depart from the principles of doing fair and honest business' was always his mantra. According to Dr Irani, on one occasion, Tata Steel even lost a mine right worth hundreds of crores, because it did not budge from its core principles of doing fair and honest business. Long-term success is built on the foundation of solid ethical values and principles.

Social Responsibility

True to the ethos of our founders, Dr Irani was always of the view that corporates should take an active role in social transformations. In 2009, Tata Group was trying to implement the Affirmative Action (AA) programme. The background to this initiative was that Manmohan Singh, the prime minister at that time, had appealed that industry should demonstrate more inclusion for SC/ST youths. Their representation was not good enough in the private sector. Dr Irani led the AA programme from the front and demonstrated extreme passion for the cause. I would always hear him saying to one of the NGO partners: 'Professor Mehta, you keep selecting deserving candidates from marginalized communities; we have the money for them.' (Tata Group commits 100 scholarships every year for boys and girls from backward communities for higher studies. This has been running for the last fifteen years through the Foundation of Academic Excellence and Access.) Dr Irani later headed a CII task force on affirmative action.

The credit for several foundational efforts for institution building also goes to Dr Irani. The sustainability and climate change programme started in Tata Group with Dr Irani at the helm. At Jamshedpur, too, he undertook many CSR initiatives that needed significant capital, such as the Mango Bridge. Jamshedpur is located on the confluence of two rivers, the Subarnarekha and

Kharkai; earlier, getting in or out of Jamshedpur was difficult. The Mango Bridge was the first four-lane bridge on the Subarnarekha River, connecting Jamshedpur to the national highway. Other such initiatives included the approach road connecting with the Tata Nagar railway station and extending drinking water and electricity services to neighbourhoods beyond the company-operated areas. Dr Irani used the principle of 'people's welfare first' in his decision-making. These were not easy decisions, as the project costs were high compared to Tata Steel's earnings at that time.

* * *

By the time Dr Irani superannuated in 2001, he had become the doyen of Indian industry, a pioneer, the beloved 'Steel Man of India'. He was recognized as a pillar in India's economic reforms and a flagbearer for India's transformational journey. Dr Irani is credited with the massive transformation of Tata Steel as it became a leading global steel company. He was instrumental in driving change across industry.

His commitment to India's growth, fuelled by his passion and ingenuity, heralded many advancements in the country. He was a mentor and guide for the industry, steering it to new heights. Dr Irani passionately supported economic reforms. He articulated progressive industry views on new policies and drove consensus among various stakeholders. He was a champion of competitiveness through quality management, sustainability, technology and globalization. He laid the foundation for affirmative action for vulnerable sections of society, setting the precedents of 'community first' and industry response in the areas of education, employment and entrepreneurship. He also shaped corporate governance and corporate social responsibility narratives for the Indian industry.

Finally, Dr Irani was an affectionate family man, and his warmth and kindness helped establish numerous friendships across the world.

I would be failing in my duty if I didn't mention Dr Irani's contribution in shaping and elevating the Business Excellence movement in Tata Group. Post 2001, after his superannuation from Tata Steel, Dr Irani was elevated as director, Tata Sons, and chairman, TQMS (currently Tata Business Excellence Group). Excellence in business has always been a virtue of Tata companies from their earliest days. But Business Excellence as a process and methodology was adopted by the company only after World War II, especially in Japan. From Japan this idea went to the USA, and it came to India in the late 1980s. Tata Steel under the stewardship of Dr Irani became a leader in adopting Business Excellence values, principles and processes. As mentioned before, TQM and TBEM were the key enablers and concepts that Dr Irani leveraged extensively in Tata Steel's transformation.

Tata Steel won the coveted JRD QV award in 2000, the first Tata company to reach this milestone. In his address during the award ceremony, Ratan Tata said, 'If someone would have asked me a few years ago which was the company least likely to win the award, I would have said Tata Steel.'

When Dr Irani came to Tata Sons as chairman, TQMS, he brought with him tremendous credibility to the subject of Business Excellence and a live example of how the concept can be leveraged. Under his leadership, many companies accelerated their Business Excellence movement and won the JRD QV award: TCS in 2004; Tata Motors' Commercial Vehicles Business unit in 2005; Titan Watch division in 2006; Tata Chemical, Tata Metaliks and the Tinplate Company of India in 2007, etc.

The Business Excellence movement, under the stewardship of Dr Irani, became a benchmark for other corporates as well.

The scope of Business Excellence also evolved under Dr Irani and embraced many emerging themes, such as innovation, climate change, affirmative action. The Tata Group, in more ways than one, has been a pioneer in the Business Excellence movement in India, and it is fair to say that the major credit for this goes to Dr Irani.

Another exciting contribution made by Dr Irani was in the field of education. In 2003, his successor, B. Muthuraman, instituted an education excellence programme and kept the highest award in the name of Dr Irani. It was called Dr Jamshed Irani Award for Education Excellence. I was again privileged to lead this initiative. Since his name was attached to this programme, Dr Irani made it a point to attend all its functions. He was of the belief that the concepts of quality and excellence had to be taught to children at the school level. The idea was that if kids were taught and trained at schools, there would not be any need for corporates to begin training their employees at the age of thirty on these subjects. Many schools in and around Jamshedpur have worked hard, embedded elements of excellence into their culture and have won the coveted Dr Irani Education Excellence Award.

Dr Irani was exceedingly pleased with his contributions to the revision of Company Law, 2005. In 2004, the Government of India had constituted an expert committee on Company Law under the chairmanship of Dr Irani. The committee's mandate was to comprehensively revise the Companies Act, 1956, and modernize it by incorporating contemporary and internationally recognized best practices. He mentioned to me that it was a monumental task and consumed a significant amount of his time. For three months, he practically resided in Delhi, dedicating his focus to this endeavour.

Another accomplishment that brought great joy to Dr Irani was receiving the Padma Bhushan in 2007. During our conversations, he mentioned that it meant a lot to him, especially since he received it from A.P.J. Abdul Kalam. Dr Iani had immense respect for Dr Kalam and always looked up to him.

* * *

I would like to share a small anecdote about Dr Irani's personality. It was 2007. Dr Irani used to sit on the fourth floor of Bombay House. Valsraj was his office secretary. One day, I barged into Dr Irani's office without a prior appointment and requested Valsraj if I could meet Dr Irani for 5–10 minutes. I wanted to have a conversation with him about some sensitive subject. After some time, when his scheduled appointment got over, I went into his chamber. I was feeling guilty for not having sought prior appointment. Unfortunately, the conversation went beyond ten minutes. Valsraj came in and reminded Dr Irani that some foreign delegates were waiting for him. Hearing him, I started getting up, but then came Dr Irani's voice: 'You please continue, you are more important.' We spoke for another ten minutes. This was typical of Dr Irani—he made the other person feel absolutely comfortable.

For this book I visited his home several times, and he would always instruct me to first get two drinks from his bar before we even began our conversation. Dr Irani followed the principles of simplicity, common sense and humility. And it has been an honour and a delight to work with him.

Dr Irani used to maintain a very detailed journal, where he would record the key events of his life and career. He was meticulous about this, and many of the anecdotes you will read in his memoir are picked up from those journal entries. He loved playing cards. (Diwali was the biggest occasion at his house for cards-playing. During the Covid days, he used to play cards with Daisy Irani, since there were only those two at home at that time.)

In his journals, he recorded every rupee he won or lost in his games of cards.

During one of my interviews with him, I asked him if he had taken account of all the money he had won and lost over the course of his entire 30–40-year career. And to my surprise, he said he had done that calculation. His words were, 'It evens out.'

'I calculated it two–three times and can say with some degree of confidence that it just evens out,' he told me. And then he added, 'Perhaps life is also like that!'

In his book *Indomitable Spirit*, A.P.J. Abdul Kalam describes an 'indomitable spirit' as having two components. The first component is that there must be a *vision*, leading to higher goals of achievement. The second component, he says, is the *ability to overcome all hurdles coming in the way*. He illustrates these with these lines by the poet–saint Thiruvalluvar:

> That whatever may be the depth of the river or lake or pond, whatever may be the condition of the water, the lily flower always comes out and blossoms. Similarly, if there is a definite determination to achieve a goal, even against insurmountable problems, you will succeed.

Having worked with Dr Irani for a long period of time, I can vouch that these two tenets of an indomitable spirit characterize him very well. Though Dr Irani is not present among us, his thoughts and principles will continue to guide us to take on the future. Like many others, I too consider him as my mentor. Dr Irani, you will not be missed, as you will always be in our heart!

One last confession. Dr Irani wanted to dictate a chapter each on Russi Mody and R.N. Tata as well. He wanted it to be the last chapters of his memoir. Unfortunately, he could not complete that wish. Dr Irani, Mr Mody and Mr Tata worked together for a very long time. He told me that Ratan Tata was very supportive and worked very closely with him for the transformation of Tata Steel. Ratan Tata's strategic vision made a huge difference to Tata Steel's transformation story.

This memoir offers a rare insight into Dr Jamshed Irani's life as a person, as a CEO, as a friend, as a technocrat and as a leader. The chapters have been sequenced in the logical progression, from childhood, youth and onwards to his life as a leader. My only recommendation to you will be to chew it slowly and enjoy it at your own pace.

Happy Reading!

N.K. Sharan
Senior vice president, TBExG, Tata Sons

PART I

MY FORMATIVE YEARS AND JOURNEY TO TATA STEEL

My Parents

When I look back, I realize my childhood was a privileged one, not quite like that of the common man in India in the middle of the twentieth century.

My father and grandfather were senior executives in what was known as Empress Mills. The 'Empress' in the name came from the fact that the Tatas started operating the mill in 1875, which was the time when Queen Victoria became empress of India. In a way, I was brought up in the Tata tradition, imbibing the values laid down by Jamsetji Tata, who himself spent considerable time in the second half of the nineteenth century at Empress Mills, the foundation of his empire. In fact, the historic Gate #1 of Empress Mills was on the same road where my father had a company-sanctioned bungalow for many years, and where I spent the first fifteen years of my life, from 1936 to 1952.

My father had joined Empress Mills at a very early age. He only had one passion in life beyond his work and family—cricket. He almost made it to the visiting Indian eleven to the United Kingdom in the late 1920s. But he had to give up his place in the squad at the last minute, because the English wanted a representation of the Indian royalty, and so my father had to make place for the maharaja of Vizianagaram. Though he missed that tour, he did play against the MCC (Marylebone Cricket Club) in what was known as Lord Tennyson's XI in the early 1930s. He left his mark on the cricket scene in Nagpur by organizing an annual tournament in the early 1940s known as the Guzder League. The name is a reminder of how personally involved he was in cricket— Guzder being the name of my maternal grandfather, who was also a keen cricketer. I have often wondered whether my father would have preferred me to progress in the world of cricket rather than become the managing director of Tata Steel!

My father retired from Empress Mills in the 1950s, and we moved out of the Empress Mills compound to a bungalow, which he had built in a very pleasant area of Nagpur known as Civil Lines. That bungalow exists to this day, but it is not in our possession, as my sister and I have sold it and have no connection with it now.

Values Imparted by My Father

My father was my best friend. Even when occasionally he criticized and disciplined me, I found him to be a great pillar of support. I remember when I was given a new cricket bat made in the UK. It quickly became my prized possession. But on the evening I used it for the first time, I ended up misusing it. I had an altercation with a friend, and I used the bat to hit him on his legs, which was obviously a very impetuous and incorrect gesture. My friend howled in pain and ran to his home, which was next door to ours. Later, when my father came to hear about my act, he took me by the hand, asked me to bring my new bat, and made me go to my friend and apologize for my nasty behaviour. He gave my precious bat to him in compensation. Of course, my friend's father intervened, and the bat came safely back to my hands. But the incident taught me that I could not take the law in my own hands, whatever the provocation.

Another time I was participating in a local billiards tournament. By the midway stage, it was obvious that I would lose, as my opponent was far ahead. In frustration, I threw my cue on the table and walked off, saying that I would not continue. My father, who was watching the game from a high seat, clambered down, made me pick up my cue and, in front of all my friends, instructed me to continue with the game till its conclusion. I, of course, lost badly. But it taught me never to walk away and to sportingly face all situations, however difficult or impossible.

My First Overseas Trip

My first overseas trip, to Europe, along with a group of Young Men's Christian Association (YMCA) members, was in keeping with my father's intentions of giving me a good education, which included an understanding of the way people lived all over the world.

We seized an opportunity which came upon us in 1952, when I was sixteen years old. I had completed my matriculation examination in April in Nagpur, and my college career was not due to begin till the end of July. In between, there was almost a four-month gap. The Bombay wing of the YMCA was organizing a trip to Europe for its members and their families. My father thought it a very good opportunity for me to see how the world outside India lived. He himself had never travelled out of India till then. So he suggested that I enrol as a member of this group of so-called youngsters (I say so-called because, though the YMCA was supposed to be for younger people, quite a few older people were also its members, and many in the group were veterans). The total cost for this two-and-a-half-month trip was Rs 5400, all expenses paid, including travel, hotels, food, sightseeing. Even considering that a dollar at that time was worth Rs 7.5 and a pound was Rs 13.5, that figure was ridiculously low for a ten-week trip to Europe. So both my parents felt that this was a good gift to me for having completed my schooling.

The group going on the trip was managed by a person named John Anthony, a live wire at YMCA, Mumbai. My father contacted him. In those days, arrangements could be made very swiftly and competently, even though there was no communication equipment of the type we have now. Before I knew it I was in Mumbai, well before the first of May that year, to make the necessary preparations. It was an easy matter to arrange the passport and all the visas. The luggage restrictions were the same as now, and my father bought me two small suitcases for all my belongings for this ten-week sojourn.

On the appointed day, 1 May, our group assembled at the Santacruz airport. We numbered about sixty, the oldest among us a seventy-year-old. The first leg of our journey was an Air India flight via Bahrain and Cairo. At Alexandria, we disembarked, because we had a two-day layover.

We took advantage of the two-day break at the Cairo Port and visited the pyramids and the Sphinx in Egypt. That was a lovely short trip, and we caught up with the plane again in Alexandria. From there, we flew to Rome, the first stop in our European trip. Even by plane, the journey was slow—eight hours each from Bombay to Bahrain and then from Bahrain to Cairo. We finally reached Rome three days after departing from Bombay.

It was my first flight, and I was quite airsick. Some of the ladies in the group kindly looked after me, reviving me from my airsickness. Thankfully, I was okay by the time we were in Cairo and could enjoy the visit to the pyramids and the Sphinx.

I recall that as we got out of the plane in Rome, one or two things struck me. The first was the large advertisements and billboards lined on either side of the highway from the Ciampino airport of Rome. At that time, we'd had no experience of advertisements of this type. And in a way, they were quite annoying, because they spoiled the view of the city as far as the passengers on the bus were concerned.

I was also struck by the security arrangements in Europe. In India, we had policemen with nothing more than a baton in their hand. And even in 1952 in Europe, the policemen were armed. Why should police carry pistols? Some even had submachine guns. It was a cultural shock.

We stayed in a hotel overlooking a large square. I don't know whether it was at the instigation of my parents, but I was clubbed in a room with a Parsi bachelor, Mr Dubash, for most of the trip. He became like a father figure to me. We were together for almost two months, and he got me out of whatever trouble I might have landed in.

We spent four good days in Rome, undertaking a thorough tour of the city during our stay—from Caesar's statue to the Vatican, to the Pope himself, whom we saw during a ceremony from a window overlooking the Vatican.

From Rome, we travelled by Italian luxurious coaches, called CIATS—something we had not seen in India before—to Naples to visit Mount Vesuvius. The museum in Pompeii, which showed people buried under the ash at the time of this volcano's eruption 2000 years ago, fascinated us. Then we were off by boat to Capri, a beautiful island, which I have been fortunate to visit several times later. But the first visit was extraordinary. I remember going up the aerial ropeway to the highest point in Capri, from where there was a sheer 2000-foot drop into the Mediterranean.

We enjoyed our two days in Capri. Then we were back by boat to Sorrento and Naples, and finally to Rome. One must remember that this was hardly six years after the war, so there were lots of telltale marks and remnants of World War II. There had been a lot of destruction in Italy.

Then we went to Florence, a beautiful city filled with artwork and architectural projects, which, fortunately, had been spared the ravages of the war. Then on to Venice and northern Italy. We went all over—from Lake Maggiore to Pisa, where I climbed up the almost 200 steps of the Leaning Tower with ease, something I would not be able to do now. But at that time, I almost ran up those 200 steps. Altogether, we spent three weeks in Italy, graced by lovely weather. I must add that it was in Italy that I developed my taste for good ice cream and chocolate. I also tasted Toblerone chocolates for the first time there and developed a taste for them, which has not left me even to this day.

During our sojourn in Italy, we were exposed to the culture of the Roman Catholic religion. I must add here that even during my schooling in Nagpur, I had learnt the catechism and read the Bible (the gospel according to St Luke and St John). This was much against my parents' wish, but I had to do it, because the catechism was a subject in the school curriculum and if one did not appear in the school exam, one would lose marks. So my parents had reluctantly agreed that I could go to church in Nagpur and learn the catechism. And funnily enough, for the five or six years that I was in a Catholic school in Nagpur, I won the prize or top marks in Catholic history every year. This stood me in good stead when we visited Italy, for I could better appreciate the Vatican through my earlier studies of the Bible.

After almost three weeks in Italy, we crossed the border into Switzerland, a completely different world for me. Having remained neutral and independent throughout World War II, Switzerland was unaffected by the devastation. We stayed in Lucerne and Interlaken, two beautiful places, visiting the mountains around there. It was here that I started my collection of keyrings. My parents had not given me much pocket money, so I was not able to buy any expensive souvenirs. But one thing that attracted me was keyrings. They were nice and light to carry, and they carried the name of the place being visited. And this hobby of collecting keyrings, which started inadvertently, has stayed with me throughout my life. Now I have a collection of keyrings from all over the world. My friends, looking at my collection, have often presented me with very pretty ones, but these mean nothing to me. My collection is based on the principle that the keyring must be from a place I have visited. So anything outside my own travels, even if it is pretty, means nothing to me. I have hundreds of keyrings at my house now.

One episode I would like to record here illustrates the honesty of the people of Switzerland. We had gone up the Jungfrau, and on the way back I had forgotten my old Kodak camera on the train. I was very sad, not because of the value of the camera but because this meant I would not be able to take photographs and record various aspects of my journey. However, I could afford to buy a new camera from the limited pocket money my father had given me. I spent a lot of it in buying a Swiss camera, an Ikon, which was a luxury in those days. I bought it two days after I had lost my camera, and as luck would have it, the Swiss people found my camera on the train. They tracked me down and handed me back that camera in Geneva. By that time, of course, I had already bought my new camera. But it shows the honesty and the thoroughness of the Swiss.

Coming back to our trip, after about ten days in Switzerland, we went into Germany, which, of course, was badly affected by the war. It was shocking, even six years after the war was over, to see cities laid absolutely bare and destroyed, unable to recover. Then we entered France, by which, of course, I mean Paris. One of the difficult tasks of the chief of YMCA was to keep the young boys away from the nightclubs of Paris. He had obviously visited them several times but never took us along. He was there with us every evening, showing us the beauty of Paris—the Eiffel Tower and other structures that had survived the ravages of war—but never the nightclubs. Hitler had not been successful in destroying Paris. We roamed over its avenues and took boat rides, drinking in its beauty.

Next on our itinerary was Brussels and then Amsterdam. Once again, beautiful cities that were still recovering from the devastating impact of World War II. From Amsterdam we continued our tour by coach, journeying to the northern countries—Copenhagen, Sweden and Norway. The northern part of Europe had not suffered much in the war.

I made it a point to climb to one of the tallest structures in the city, wherever I was—whether it was Copenhagen, Stockholm, Oslo or Amsterdam—so that I could view the city below me. It was the quickest and simplest way to see as much as possible, but it was obviously hard on the legs, and I could only do it because I was sixteen at the time. I would not be able to do anything like that now.

Overall, we travelled through various capitals of Europe, each more beautiful than the other.

One incident from that time comes to my mind. We were travelling in Norway by train and went to the train restaurant for our lunch. While we were eating there, fully unaware of what was happening, the front part of the train, where our passenger seats were, had been disconnected. We tried to get back to our seats, but we only saw the rails. A portion of the train had been uncoupled; we were in one half, and our baggage and our friends were in the other. Despite that, there was no confusion. The travel people were very efficient. They put us through various alternative links, and by evening we were reconnected with our baggage and our friends in Oslo.

Once again, the difference in the speed and efficiency of communication was remarkable. One evening, when we were in a remote part of Norway, with literally very few communication links, I was happy to see a telegram directed to me from my parents telling me that I had passed my high school examination in first class. This was just a simple telegram, sent from Nagpur and delivered to me in the Scandinavian city of Gothenburg within a matter of hours, if not minutes.

After the Scandinavian portion of our trip, we went to Glasgow and then to London. One interesting fact is that, while we were in England, we were given coupons with which we could buy chocolates and other luxury items, as we were looked upon as tourists. These same items were not available to the local public, even though the war had ended seven years earlier—the economies of these countries were so badly shattered that only two decades later would the local people get back to normal life.

Mr Dubash, the old gentleman with whom I shared my room for most of the journey, was well versed with London and would regale us with tales about his student days there, in the 1920s. In London, too, we did all the usual touristy things—went down the Thames River, visited parks, visited the zoo, visited Buckingham Palace, where we even had a chance to catch sight of Queen Elizabeth on the balcony. Fortunately, the museums, in Europe had survived the war, and all the treasures had been well preserved. Hitler and his forces had not been able to destroy the emblems of several civilizations.

After two months, all of May and most of June, we finished our sojourn in London and journeyed to Southampton to catch our ship back to India, a journey of eighteen days. I shared a cabin with four young people on that journey back and thoroughly enjoyed myself. From Gibraltar, we re-entered the Mediterranean, which is a very calm sea, and stopped in Algiers, which was then ruled by the French. Algiers was a city full of traders, and at that time, there was no terrorism and no hatred between Muslims and Christians. From Algiers, we sailed further east, to the Suez Canal. Even then, the Suez Canal had started becoming a site of uncertainty. The ship party was told to keep a low profile and preferably stay in their cabins and not roam around too freely on the decks, because there was always the chance of an occasional outlaw taking pot shots at the passengers on the ship. The Suez Canal, as it's well known, is a very narrow strip of water. And indeed, as our ship passed through, we could easily throw a stone from the deck on to either side of the canal.

Several Parsi families from India had established ties in Aden, and we could visit some of those during our short stopovers. After Aden we crossed the Arabian Sea to Mumbai, which we reached on 13 July, exactly two and a half months after we had left Mumbai, starting our journey.

Thus ended a very pleasurable two and a half months, a gift from my parents which certainly broadened my outlook. Their objective was not to give me a pleasure trip but to give me an exposure to the rest of the world. In that objective, they were eminently successful. I owe a lot of gratitude to them for their sacrifice in allowing me to visit large tracts of Europe even before they had made any trips outside India.

My First Encounters with the City
of Jamshedpur

When I first visited Jamshedpur, I was not connected to Tata Steel in any way. I was a student of geology at Nagpur University, and a group of us, led by a professor at Nagpur University, made a study tour of the region around the city. We came by the overnight train from Nagpur and spent that first night on the railway platform at the Chotanagpur station. We were to catch a train to the Tata Steel mines at Gurumasani early next morning. So, arriving after dark at Chotanagpur, we had some sort of a meal at the railway station and then elected to spend the night on the platform. After a couple of days at the mines, we took the train back to Tata Nagar and stayed at the Maharastra Mandal guest house in Bistupur for another two days, visiting the steel plant and other associated facilities in Jamshedpur. Little did I know at that time that one day Jamshedpur would become my home and I would spend a large part of my life in this city.

My next brush with Jamshedpur was not an actual visit; it was the subject of a conversation—we were discussing my future. I was about to leave for further studies abroad. My parents and I, as a matter of courtesy, had asked my grandmother for her blessings before I departed for Sheffield. During the conversation, my grandmother asked my parents where 'Jumpsu'—as she called me—would work. She was very insistent that I must come back after spending two or three years studying in the UK. She also advised me, or rather my parents, that on my return I could go to any place in India to make a living, except that one place which she had never visited but about which she had heard many nasty remarks and rumours—Jamshedpur. She had never visited Jamshedpur but had read about it in Gujarati papers. And apparently, the old lady was not impressed by the goings-on in that city. Of course, the good old soul departed from this world well before I could settle down in Jamshedpur. She passed away in Nagpur just before I left for my studies in Sheffield.

Early Connections with Tata Group and Tata Steel

As I have mentioned earlier, I grew up in the shadow of Empress Mills, which was one of India's primary spinning and weaving companies at the time and Jamsetji Tata's first organized large-scale venture. My father and my maternal grandfather both worked there for their whole lifetime. And, in fact, the chimneys of the mill loomed over the house where I stayed. Though my grandfather passed away when I was a little baby, I stayed for fifteen years in that house, a stone's throw from Empress Mills's main gate.

Still, I personally had no attachments to the house of Tata, and I could have landed up wherever I wished. It just so happened that around 1956 or 1957, I got a scholarship from the J.N. Tata Endowment for the Higher Education of Indians. I was one of the 10–12 people they selected every year. My batchmate, by the way, was Jayant Narlikar, the famous astrophysicist. The scholarship was partly a gift, with the majority to be paid back after we started working, though there was no commitment that I had to join the house of Tata.

So, with my scholarship money, I went on to pursue my higher studies in metallurgy in Sheffield. This was around 1958, when the steel industry was coming up in India and plants such as the ones in Bhilai, Durgapur and Rourkela were being built. If I may say so, I did rather well, winning a gold medal and so on. A lady by the name of Pilloo Vesugar used to look after the scholars. After we passed out, she wrote to me with some news. The team had put up a report of how the various scholarship winners had performed and had it sent to J.R.D. Tata. When he read about me in this report, he wrote in the margin, 'If ever this young man wishes to come back to India, he should first knock on the doors of the Tata Iron and Steel Company.' Mrs Vesugar added that JRD had never done anything like this for any of the other scholars, and now that he had written as much for me, I should count it as a great privilege and follow what he had said. So, I said, okay.

After studying metallurgy as a postgraduate student for two years, I worked as a doctorate research scholar from 1960–63. Studies done, I started working at the British Iron and Steel Research Association (BISRA). Not long after I joined BISRA, sometime around 1963, I came on a holiday to India. I visited Bombay House, as per the advice I had been given, but JRD was out of the country at that time. Mr Moolgaokar, who was the vice chairman, saw me and assured me that he would arrange a visit for me to Jamshedpur. Accordingly, I booked my train tickets from Nagpur, where I was staying with my parents, to Jamshedpur. Sir Joe Ghandy and the Kutar brothers were the bosses in Jamshedpur at that time.

I stayed in the city for 3–4 days, exploring it. It made me happy to see such a clean place in India. I had put up at the Tisco hotel, and I remember that on the last evening, I walked back from the general office to my room. On the way, at the junction of C Road and Office Road, was a culvert. I sat on it, and all that had happened in the past couple of days ran past my mind's eye.

I thought, 'Well, Jamshedpur is not such a bad place to be in, if ever I think of coming back to India.'

And that was the first link I had with Tata Steel, apart from the fact that my family members were employed in Empress Mills. Oddly enough, the date is implanted in my mind, 22 November 1963, not because of this passing thought, but because on that very day the American President John F. Kennedy was assassinated in Dallas. I heard about the assassination on the train journey back to Nagpur.

A Series of Interviews

When I went back to Sheffield, I started a correspondence with JRD, negotiating for a position in Tata Steel. He remembered my report from the J.N. Tata endowment. And I had previously met S. Moolgaokar, the vice chairman of Telco and Tisco. All this led JRD to arranging a meeting with me and S.K. Nanavati, who was then the director-in-charge at Jamshedpur.

I had a series of rather unusual interviews, maybe because I was located in a faraway land at the time. I think it is very rare that a candidate is interviewed in his own office and the managing director of the company travels to meet up with him. But that was what happened and when S.K. Nanavati visited the UK; he travelled from London to Sheffield to interview me in my office. I remember I was a bit embarrassed to be sitting in my office and being interviewed by the chief of Tata Steel in Jamshedpur. He even took me to the hotel bar later that evening, and we spent time discussing what I would likely encounter if I made the move from Sheffield to Jamshedpur.

The meeting obviously went well, because Tata Steel made me an offer. The deal was not done overnight. For some time we corresponded about what I would be doing and so on. And in 1967, I finally decided that I would join Tata Steel on a lien basis.

The BISRA was happy to give me a lien for one year on my job. They said they would welcome me back within a year if I decided that I would come back from India.

Joining Tata Steel

I landed up in Jamshedpur in early January 1968. I was appointed assistant to the director of Research and Development, Dr B.G. Paranjape. Unfortunately, my first few months in Jamshedpur were very discouraging, because of the atmosphere which prevailed in the R&D department in Tata Steel. I found myself in an ego clash with the director, who didn't trust me with anything nor give me any responsibilities. I was just visiting the department aimlessly.

I had taken the precaution of coming to Jamshedpur on a one-year lien from Sheffield, with my employers there ready to welcome me back should my early experiences in Tata Steel prove disappointing. That had indeed turned out to be the case, and around April–May, I decided that I would exercise my option and go back to BISRA. I had even written out my letter of resignation, indicating that I would be going back, and given it to Mr Chander, who was the general manager. Nothing happened. The feeling was that if I wanted to go, they couldn't hold me back.

This was when JRD played a role in shaping my career for the second time. He had come to Jamshedpur on one of his regular visits. When he visited the R&D department, he spotted me. I had met him before coming to Jamshedpur, so he knew what I looked like. Seeing me, he walked over and said, 'Hello, young man. How are things going with you?'

'Not so well, sir,' I said. And I recounted to him my experiences and told him that I was thinking of going back after the lien period was over. All he said was 'Oh' before walking away. Well, that was it, I told myself. I could stick with my plan of going back.

Next morning, when I drove up to the R&D laboratory, everyone there was looking for me. I had stopped at one or two plants on the way, so I was a bit late. It was around 10.30 a.m., and I was told to go to the general office immediately. As soon as I reached, I was ushered into a room, which, by the way, was the same one I would occupy for twenty years as my office—on the first floor.

The three Tata Steel directors—S.K. Nanavati, director-in-charge, Russi Mody, director in charge of raw materials, and R.S. Pandey, director in charge of administration—were waiting for me. Obviously, JRD had had a word with them and inquired about what was wrong and what they could do. After they heard my story, they said that it was June and I still had another six months to go before my lien was over. They told me they would give me another posting, and since I had a few months, I could try that out and see how things went.

The next day I was transferred out of the R&D department and placed in the general superintendent's office as assistant to S. Viswanathan, the general superintendent at that time. And there my experience was totally different. He gave me all sorts of responsibilities and encouraged me, and within 2–3 months, I had changed my mind and written to my people in Sheffield saying that I would not be returning to BISRA. So that was the second time JRD intervened in my career. The first concerned my appointment itself.

I was moved around a lot between 1968 and 1974, gaining much experience. It was also an important period of my life, because I got married in 1971. I became the assistant general superintendent in 1974, and, as they say, the rest is history. I have no regrets that I chose to stay back with the Tatas.

Daisy and My Home in Jamshedpur

Daisy Siganporia entered my life when I was already thirty-two years old. I had only recently returned from my ten-year stay in Sheffield. I had moved into one of the Kaiser Bungalows in Jamshedpur, and for the first year or two that I was there, we hardly met. Both our fathers were ardent free masons, and we frequently attended masonic parties. We met at one of these. And after that, our benevolent friends made sure that we met frequently at parties, dinners and picnics.

I cannot say that we had common interests. Daisy loved dancing, and I had no interest in that activity. I love sports, and I'm not sure whether Daisy had any liking for sports. But we had a friendship. And we continued to meet during her vacations from her studies in Chennai. Friendship turned to interest. Interest turned to liking, and liking turned to love. Our only common interest, to start with, were the movies at the Beldih Club, and people started noticing that Jamshed Irani, who was looked upon as a loner, had started bringing the same girl to the club, movies and other activities. They had guessed correctly—there was something more than friendship in the air. To cut a long story short, I proposed to Daisy on a moonlit night in Dimna, and we were both thrilled when she said yes. Both sets of parents were also happy.

From my proposal in March 1971, things moved fast. We had planned for the wedding in December, but it so happened that in May I was told that I would be attending an international conference in Brussels in September. I joked with Daisy that she could come with me, and we could have our wedding festivities as planned in December. Obviously, both sets of parents were totally opposed to that idea, and marriage plans were advanced into September, so that we could spend our honeymoon abroad. We got married on 17 September at the Beldih Club in the new hall. Our wedding was the first function there.

The conference would not have allowed us to stay abroad for more than a week, but thanks to the fact that I had parked some retirement funds in a bank in Sheffield, and which I could immediately withdraw, we had ample funds to travel through Europe. We started with London and Paris, and went on to many places in Switzerland and Italy. We left the European continent after a month and stopped in Iran, which was under the Shah's regime at that time, on the way back. We spent three or four days there, visiting places of Zoroastrian interest, and finally landed back in Mumbai in the first week of November.

In those early days we survived on a stringent budget, which amounted to about Rs 1000 a month—this was for me, Daisy and our dog, Liza, who had entered my life before Daisy! Finances were tight, but love saw us through. Zubin was born on 11 August 1972, well before the first anniversary of our marriage. We continue to stay at the 28 Inner Circle Road, Kaiser Bungalow, where a third bedroom and some air conditioners were added to make life more comfortable. Daisy had previously held a job at a bank but had given up on it. Right from the start, we had decided that we would live on my earnings, and Daisy would be free to do some social work and, of course, look after our baby boy, Zubin. He was followed by Niloufer, two and a half years later, and another two and a half years later, we had the pleasure of welcoming Tanaaz, who was a happy, golden-haired 13-pound baby. The six of us, including Liza, lived very happily in our Kaiser Bungalow for five years.

By that time, my career had taken off, and I got several promotions in quick succession. It was generally accepted and recognized in the steel company that I was destined for higher responsibilities. However, it came as a shock when, in early 1978—Tanaaz being only a few months old—I was instructed by Russi Mody to move my residence to a house next to his own. It so happened that one of the local politicians, Mr Sarangi, had demanded and was refused a Tata Steel accommodation by Russi Mody. The politician was enraged and was heard to comment that he would forcibly occupy the bungalow next to Mr Mody's. It was vacant at the time, because the previous occupant, Mr Nanavati, had left, and no one had moved in. On hearing Mr Sarangi's comment, Mr Mody called me to his office and said that he wanted me to move into that empty bungalow the very next day!

I had a look at the bungalow, which was in a very poor state, not having been occupied for a long time. The windows and internal doors were missing, and, in general, the rooms were in a dilapidated condition. I pleaded with Mr Mody and told him about my inability to move into such a bungalow. But he would not hear any excuses. He called Mr Bodhanwala, the chief engineer at that time, and instructed him to get one room and a bathroom ready overnight. All resources were called in, and within a couple of days, a room was made comfortable and operational. Into that one room I moved with Daisy, our three children and our dog, Lisa. The reward, of course, was that Mr Mody himself began to take a personal interest in renovating the rest of the house while we resided in that one corner. He visited almost every day to see the renovation work and gave instructions to the contractors on what was to be done. So, in a way, we were fortunate that the house was renovated under Mr Mody's patronage, and everything that we desired was done over the following 6–8 months to make 3 C Road a very liveable accommodation.

What had started off as an emergency measure culminated in the setting up of a very fine house in which Daisy, I and our children spent twenty-seven happy years. We did not have to move from that house till my retirement.

Lisa passed away a few years after we moved into 3 C, and she was followed by two other boxers, who were succeeded by two pugs. All five were buried in our 3 C Road garden. After that, we thought we were too old to look after dogs.

Daisy was of immense help to me, and I must recognize her contribution in my rise to the number one position in Tata Steel in Jamshedpur. Let me give a case in point. I had developed a system where the man in charge of personnel at that time, Dr Jitu Singh, would prepare a review of my performance by consulting with 20–25 of my closest colleagues. They were expected to give their opinion anonymously, and Jitu would collate the information. He would then summarize the results and pass them on to me without disclosing who said what. It was sufficient for me to know how I was performing in the eyes of my closest colleagues. I remember one occasion when my close friend N.P. Sinha openly said that as far as human relationships were concerned, he would rate me at zero, but that did not matter because he would rate Mrs Irani in the highest possible bracket! This pleased me no end. Daisy was holding up her position and then helping me administer my job. Her popularity and effectiveness were as important to me as my own in our organization.

My Parents' Last Years

My parents would often visit me in Jamshedpur, which was just an overnight train journey from Nagpur, where they had settled after retirement. They were with me on 26 March 1974. My father, who was quite fit, drove me to office at around eight in the morning. After that he went back home and had a reasonable breakfast; then he placed his grandson Zubin in a pram and went for a walk. It was his morning ritual to take Zubin on an outing. When he came back home one morning, at around ten, he complained to Daisy that he was feeling a little uneasy. Daisy informed our good friend Dr Anklesaria, who was the chief physician at Tata Main Hospital (TMH) at the time. He advised Daisy to bring my father to TMH, which she did immediately. By 11 a.m., the doctors were examining my father. Almost exactly then, he had a massive heart attack. In 1974, TMH did not have ICU facilities, except for the bare minimum, one bed in the medical ward. Though the doctor tried to revive my father, there was nothing to be done, and he pronounced my father dead just after 1 p.m. By that time Daisy had called me, and I was there with her at the hospital.

For my father, it was a wonderful end—no illness, no pain, no disability till that last day. But for the family, it was a tremendous shock. I remember calling my sister, who was in Nagpur. She could not believe what had happened. She travelled overnight, and, as per Zoroastrian custom, we buried him in our Parsi graveyard, next to the Subarnarekha River, by midday on 27 March.

On looking back, I think it was a wonderful end for a wonderful person. No suffering, no pain, no ailments. Fully in his senses right up to the last moment. I do not think anyone can ask for a better end.

In contrast, my mother had an extremely difficult and almost torturous last few years, alternating between hospital and home for almost six to seven years. After my father passed away in 1974, my mother insisted on continuing to live in our Nagpur home, which was named Persepolis. My sister Diana and brother-in-law Rustom stayed with her in Persepolis. But with time, she required more and more medical attention that we could provide for her better in Jamshedpur. Initially, she alternated between Nagpur and Jamshedpur, but for the last six or seven years of her life, she was confined to bed and alternated between a cabin in the new ward at TMH and our home on C Road. By the 1990s, I was in a very senior position in Tata Steel, and my mother received great attention from the medical fraternity at the hospital.

A patient of Alzheimer's, my mother's dementia worsened month by month. Since she could not take care of herself, she needed a nurse or an attendant around the clock. Daisy was the one who paid the most attention to my mother and took on the brunt of looking after her, even though at that time her own parents (who, fortunately, were in much better health) had joined us in Jamshedpur.

With time, my mother reached a state where she could not recognize anybody except me and Daisy. She stopped recognizing even my sister, who visited from Nagpur from time to time. I do not know how aware my mother was of her own medical condition. Towards the end, which came in 1997, she was quite incoherent. Alzheimer's had taken its full toll on her, and she was put on life support. Finally, my sister came over and jointly decided that it would be better to take her off life support—our mother was physically and mentally incapable of living on her own. It was a painful decision, but one we had to take. She passed away within the next few hours.

My experiences with my parents were thus poles apart. My father had an enjoyable and healthy life right till the end, but the last few years of my mother's life were extremely difficult. I certainly have no doubts about which way is preferable.

Learning from J.R.D. Tata

A Man of Strong Principles

JRD was a man of principles, very strong principles, and I wish to recount one or two stories here in that connection.

He never spent any of the company's money. During all the chairmanships that he had of the Tata Group, he never made the company spend money on anything for his own personal use, including his office. His office was visited by many important people—by politicians and sometimes prime ministers too, who wanted to call on the chief of the House of Tata, and of course, by the bosses of Indian business. And since he never spent money on the office, it started looking a bit tatty. I remember Darbari Seth and Mr Moolgaonkar and his other colleagues, who had far more plusher offices in Bombay House, telling JRD that he must do something to improve the look of his office—after all, he was representing the House of Tata.

So, after a lot of pressure, JRD decided he must do something about his office using his own personal funds. His curtains were shabby, and the tapestry was not very appropriate, so he took the measurements and went off with his secretary to the market. Wherever he liked some tapestry, he would ask for the price. The measurements that he had acquired for his office were in his hands. He would take out a small red calculator, count how much it would cost and say, 'No, no, too expensive!' And that went on for the whole afternoon. They visited 4–5 furniture stores and came back to Bombay House without having made any purchase at all, because he felt those curtains and tapestries were too expensive.

He did not own his house, where he stayed for over half a century; nor was it owned by Tata. It belonged to the Avabai F. Petit Residuary Estate Trust, who had given it on a long lease. So he had no house in Bombay and a very simple office.

I have another story about his principled approach to life. When I was in Mumbai for work, we used to meet for lunch in Bombay House every day, with all the directors of Tata Sons or some other VIPs. One day, he came to lunch, despondent that he had lost his favourite pen. He used to carry a Parker pen set—a fountain pen and a ballpoint. 'Look,' he said, 'I have lost the ballpoint. I don't know where it has gone. I have looked all over, I got people to look in my office, my home. It's gone.' And he showed us the pen that formed the other half of the set. I made a note of it.

A few weeks later I was in London. With some difficulty, in a small shop next to Selfridges, I found the ballpoint identical to the one JRD had lost. I immediately bought it, and the next time I saw him in his office, I presented that pen to him.

JRD was delighted. 'Yes, Jamshed, it is exactly like the one I lost.' For the first one or two minutes, he used it and tried it out, but then I saw his expression change slowly. After a minute or two, he gave it back to me. He said, 'Thank you for the thought. This is exactly what I wanted, but I cannot accept it.'

'Why?' I asked. 'I thought you were looking for this.'

He said, 'Yes, but it's a principle of mine not to accept any gifts from any of my colleagues. If I did, then I know my colleagues would try to outdo each other and give me exorbitant gifts.'

'But, sir,' I said, 'nobody would know that I've given you this pen. You can say that you found it again in your room. I'm not going to go around saying that I've given JRD an identical pen.'

He said, 'Jamshed, I know you will not do any such thing. But I would know. I would know that I accepted this gift against my principles. I'm sorry, but I cannot accept it.'

I still have that pen on my table here. This was the strength of the principles he held.

After JRD died, Jim Sethna and others made an inventory of his possessions. His personal wealth was nothing, absolutely nothing, and yet JRD controlled the Tata Group.

First, Be a Good Human Being

One thing JRD insisted on was that before you could be considered good at anything (a good engineer, a good lawyer, a good doctor or, for that matter, good at any profession), you have to be a good human being. People should respect you for your human qualities rather than for any position you may hold. Many have written about this quality of JRD's. Without repeating, I would like to highlight one or two instances I observed myself, illustrating what a good human being he was.

The first event I recall occurred during a dinner at my home in Jamshedpur. JRD was the chief guest, and all the senior officers of the company and their wives were present. My old mother, eighty-plus at the time, was living with us. She was sitting quietly in a corner, where no one paid her the slightest attention. Then Daisy came into the room and announced that dinner was ready. She invited JRD to come to the dining room. But instead of going with Daisy, he walked straight up to my mother and led her by the hand. He accompanied her to the dining table, made her sit down, and made her feel important and happy.

No one would have expected that JRD would pay attention to an old lady. It was a very humane gesture, which nobody else, including me, had even thought about. It touched me.

There is one other instance I recollect that brought out his human qualities. One morning, I had gone to meet him when he was in Jamshedpur. And as a matter of formality, I said, 'Did you have a good night?'

'No, not at all,' he said. 'I was frozen the whole night. The air conditioner was too efficient, and I could not find the switch to turn it off.'

When I heard this I said, 'Sir, there is your bearer.' We had an old bearer called Sahibjan, who always used to sleep just outside his room on the veranda. 'Why didn't you ask him to do this?'

He said, 'Yes, I did think of it. But when I went out to the veranda, he was sleeping so soundly that I did not feel like waking him up.'

That was just how he was. He suffered the whole night in the cold, out of his concern for another individual.

Another, more personal, instance highlights his thoughtfulness towards others. It is well known that towards the early 1990s, I had a problem with one or two people in the management. And, in fact, there was some doubt about whether I would continue at Tata Steel. I would not relent on certain principles and had decided to rather leave than become party to activities I did not believe in.

The only time you could have a chat with JRD was late in the evening, just before he left for home. So I was sitting outside his office, thinking about what to say to him. When he came out, he saw me waiting for him. He walked over to me, put his hand on my knee and said, 'Look, Jamshed, I know what your problem is. I have been through many such situations in my career with many such executives. You trust me.'

I said, 'Sir, of course I trust you.'

'In that case,' he said, 'forget about it. I will solve your problems.'

Over the next few days and weeks, he did solve my problem. And he did exactly the same thing with Daisy. When he was in Jamshedpur after his cataract operation, Daisy would go and put eye drops in his eyes. So when she was with him, he assured her too, telling her not to worry.

As these stories show, he was always very concerned about others and tried to put people at ease.

Perfectionist to the Core

Another thing JRD was very particular about was general maintenance. He was a perfectionist. I recall an incident when he was to attend a meeting in my office, which was on the first floor. This was the layout of our general office: as soon as you entered the building, there was a staircase leading up to a landing with a bust of the founder, Jamsetji Tata. Another short flight of steps led up to the first floor, where the offices of the managing director and other directors were located.

JRD never used the lift. He always climbed the staircase, paying his respects to the founder's bust, and then went wherever it was necessary for him to go. On this occasion, I was preparing for my meeting with him in my office. So I was not with him, but my principal executive officer (PEO) was guiding him. As usual, he went up to the bust of the founder to pay his respects, but on looking around, he said, 'You can't even look after the founder's statue. It's dirty, and there are pinholes in it.' He kept on muttering in a disgusted manner.

When he came to my office, he didn't tell me anything, but my PEO took me aside and told me what had transpired. I quickly went to the next room and phoned the person who was in charge of our model room. He was an expert in rectifying minor defects, and I told him to drop everything that he was doing at present, just drop it, come to the general office and make sure that that bust was absolutely clean and perfect. If there were any holes, I said, repair them. He was to ensure everything was perfect. I gave him two hours because that was how long my meeting with JRD was supposed to last. Then I rejoined the meeting, and we carried on as normal.

After the end of the meeting, he wanted to walk down the staircase again. So I took him to the bust and, in an innocent way, said, 'Sir, I heard you have seen some defects. I'm sorry, but can you show those to me?'

He said, 'Yes, yes, Jamshed, you can't even look after the founder's bust. Disgusting!' And he went up to the bust. He looked around the bust but couldn't find any stains. There were no pinholes. JRD was really confused. And then, the shrewd person that he was, he took his fingers behind and under the bust and felt wet paint on his fingers. Then he exploded, 'You were trying to make a fool of an old man! You will never succeed in doing that!' But he was very happy that we had acted promptly and had the bust cleaned.

You could not fool him easily. He was very smart and very sincere at whatever he wanted to do. He was my professional godfather.

Part II

BUILDING TATA STEEL

Modernization Story 1: New Bar and Rod Mill

When he was on one of his visits to Jamshedpur, I told J.R.D. Tata that unless we found the money to modernize, both he and I would be standing at the gates of Tata Steel and selling tickets to see the Steel Museum, because that's what we would become. He laughed, but the message went home. Through his friends in Nissho Iwai, he arranged a visit to Japan for me. At that time, Japan was the pride of the steel industry, and I spent the month visiting all the newest Japanese plants—from blast furnaces to steel melting shops and rolling mills, from Hokkaido in the north to Kyushu in the south. A Japanese interpreter was attached to me for the entire month, so there were no communication problems.

Technologically, Japan held no surprises. What surprised me was the financial ability of the Japanese to knock down plants which were only ten years old, and find the money and the resources to build new plants on top of these 'outdated' ones. We, on the other hand, were continuing with our thirty-, forty- or even fifty-year-old units. Making improvements and improvising was our forte—'producing new wine from old bottles' was our favourite refrain—because all our plants were old, and we were trying to produce modern steel from those old units. People such as Dr Mukherjee, Dr Amit Chatterjee and others were at the forefront of turning out newer and newer steel from older and older plants. When I came back to India, I told J.R.D. Tata he should send his financial experts with me to Japan the next time! Once again, Mr Tata had a good laugh, but my message went home.

Of course, one of the reasons the Japanese could build those plants was that their banks were very supportive, and they encouraged debt-to-equity ratio of 8:1, even 10:1, in their steel companies, whereas in India we were stuck to a maximum 'safe' ratio of 2 :1. We had a pricing problem too, as the Government of India controlled the prices entirely. These government-imposed financial restrictions meant we could not sell steel at the prices that were necessary and globally traded. Technically, we were competent; financially, we were handicapped.

Once we started moving into the 1980s, Mr Tata took the initiative to start some modernization programmes. India had started opening up, and we could get small amounts of foreign exchange sanctioned. I used to visit Delhi almost twice a week for financial discussions in those days. Luckily, we had aircraft which would take me from Jamshedpur to Delhi and bring me back the same day.

We started with a very small programme, which was to set up a bar and rod mill that would make long products. We had decided that making flat products would be more difficult than making long products, because of more stringent quality requirements. Long products, like bars and rods, could be made from steel that was not so high in quality. Thus the decision to start with a bar and rod mill.

After evaluation, we finally gave the project to a British company, Davys. That is a story in itself, because their competitors, Ashlow, were also in the bidding, and they lowered the price for the mill to very low levels in the hope of getting the order. But I knew that you must pay a price for the quality you want, and that belief proved to be correct, because after we gave the order to Davys, Ashlow went bankrupt and had to close down.

The project was relatively small, worth only Rs 80 crore, but in the early 1980s, it was a lot of money. We had fixed the date of commissioning for 3 March 1982, well in advance, to make sure that everyone was on the same page. Everyone, of course, cooperated, but there were problems, and the final issue arose when one day in January our engineers came to us and said that we really could not start the mill on 2 March. I asked why, and they explained that there was a special oil for the gearbox of the new mill which was being transported from England. The ship it was on was stuck in Colombo, and there was no way to get the ship to Bombay on time. So out-of-the-box thinking was necessary. I asked them, 'Do we have this sort of mill anywhere else?' The answer was, yes. We had recently acquired a bar and rod mill at Tarapore, with the acquisition of a company called Special Steels. 'All right,' I said. 'Shut that mill down, drain the gearbox oil there and transport it to Jamshedpur.' People thought that I was a little mad, but in the end it was done. That oil was transported to Jamshedpur and put into our new gearbox, and the mill started exactly on time on 2 March. Once you are determined to do something, you can always find ways and means to do it.

Mr Tata and others came in and inaugurated the mill, and as far as I know, it is still in operation and running very well.

Modernization Story 2:
New Blast Furnace

I will now move on to the case of a new blast furnace. Now, blast furnaces cost a lot. But we learnt one day that there was a blast furnace just sitting in its packaging somewhere in Portugal. A Portuguese company with a majority government stake had ordered a blast furnace from the Italian company Italimpianti, but before they could set it up in Portugal, the European Union (EU) passed a diktat saying that if Portugal wanted to join the EU, no additional steel capacity could be set up, because Europe was overflowing with steel. To the Portuguese government, sacrificing a blast furnace was a small price to pay to join the EU.

When we came to know that this blast furnace was available in Lisbon, S.L. Srivastava, our chief engineer, and I visited the city. We saw the blast furnace and negotiated a very low price—$3 million—because the Portuguese were willing to throw it away. There were not many customers for a million-tonne blast furnace, particularly when the steel world was running well below capacity!

We shipped the furnace in three ships to Paradip. On entering port, we had to pay the usual customs duty. The customs officers

44

thought that we had paid somewhere through other means and that this low price was not the actual price. They called me and interrogated me continuously for ten hours in Bhubaneshwar. I had to answer all sorts of questions, write down my answers and sign each of them. I had no problem doing so, because I was describing exactly what had happened. I was telling the truth and had nothing to hide. Ultimately, customs released the furnace, and we brought the components to Jamshedpur.

J.R.D. Tata was in Jamshedpur at the time, and we did the bhumi puja for setting up the furnace in his presence. When JRD asked how long it would take to make it operational, I said we could do it in less than three years. He retorted, 'Jamshed, you will never be able to do that. You have no experience in this, a new blast furnace. We have not built a blast furnace for forty years. How will you do it in three years?' We took on the challenge.

Language was a major problem. The Italians had built the furnace, and the Portuguese were the customers. So, all the instructions and guidelines were in those two languages. But then we had good engineers. I particularly remember one—Amar Dhillon. Amar took charge of the stoves required to run the blast furnace. They were of a sophisticated nature, and we had not experienced such equipment before, but he took on the challenge. He and his engineers not only put up the stoves but also commissioned them.

We were able to stick to our promise and inaugurate the blast furnace in less than three years, beating the deadline by three days! When the time came for the inauguration (blowing in) of the blast furnace, Russi Mody, who was in Europe, was not available. So J.R.D. Tata himself came down from Bombay to Jamshedpur, and we inaugurated it 'on time'. The two plaques are still exhibited on the G Blast Furnace—one carrying the date of the bhumi puja and the other carrying the date of the inauguration.

We did not have any contract with Italimpianti or the Portuguese after they sold us the furnace. To get a furnace of that magnitude, and that complexity, and work on schedule without any foreign advice—it was an example of not only our determination to stick to our timelines but also our willingness to give freedom to our engineers to do the things they had not done before. That furnace is still in service and has given us very good results.

Modernization Story 3: Stamp-Charged Coke Oven Battery

We are blessed with large deposits of medium-quality coking coal In India. But prime-quality coking coal, which is required to make good quality coke, an essential raw material in the steelmaking process, is not easily available. Tata Steel, too, has ample sources of high-ash, medium-quality coking coal, but none of the prime variety, which has to be imported.

The process of washing the ash down to get coal of suitable quality presents a lot of technological problems. Without getting too technical—for making coke, coal is normally sprayed from the top of the coke oven into the oven, and because of the spraying process the density of the coal is not kept as high as it could be. Other techniques, too, don't give the coal the high density that is required for making good-quality coke. Sometime in the early 1980s, I read that there was a technique available to improve coke quality by increasing the density of coal through a process known as 'stamp charging' of coal. A firm in Germany (this was not a steel firm but a power generating unit), called SIP (Saarberg Interplan, Gmbh), had developed a process to increase the density of coal. They had adapted a technology for their power plant where they would make cakes of coal rather than use the spraying technique.

I went to SIP, I remember, on a wintry evening. Their top engineer knew as little English as I did German, but we managed to communicate. I told him that as a steel plant we were interested in their technology. Could they help us in making similar coke ovens? Egbert Harion was their chief commercial manager, and he and I struck up a partnership. Both of us made several visits to each other's plants. Our technical people were not really convinced that this would work, so I formed a team of technical experts, including Mr Kapadia, who oversaw our blast furnaces, and Dr Majumdar, who was in charge of our coke ovens. I sent them for a couple of weeks to Germany to study the process, and they came back with a thumbs-up sign. Yes, they said, we might be able to make this type of oven and hopefully make better coke. But obviously, we had a lot of preliminary work to do, largely related to the type of coal we had and must use for any coke-making technology.

Tata Steel then had six coke oven batteries. It was a risk to change them all to the new technology, so we selected one, which was due for rebuilding. We chose the coke oven battery number 7. It took us two years to adapt to the stamp-charging process. When we finally did it and started the battery, it was not a runaway success. There were quite a few challenges to be dealt with. It was a matter of getting to know the process. After a year or so of experimenting, we figured it out. Then, we quickly changed all the other batteries to the new technology—'quickly' means it took us ten years to change all the other batteries to the stamp-charging technology. We can now get good-quality coke from our own low-quality coal.

This was a big price advantage, which, in turn, helped us in making Jamshedpur a low-cost producer of steel. Of course, now newer plants have come up there, and some of them are probably better than ours, but at that time, we were the lowest-cost producer. Once again, this innovation was a matter of adopting technology to suit our local conditions.

Modernization Story 4: Innovating the Oxygen Blowing Process

After we incorporated coke ovens, it was time to start making steel the modern way—oxygen-blown. At that time, the early 1970s, a new process for oxygen blowing had been invented in Germany. It was known as the OBM process. It involves oxygen being blown into the iron bath, a crucible-like equipment to melt iron, from below; whereas conventionally, in the Linz-Donawitz (LD) process, oxygen is blown from the top.

This was another subject where JRD, even though he didn't come from a technical background, showed his acumen in making the right technical decision. Our technical people, including myself, Dr Mukherjee and Dr Amit Chatterjee, were in favour of adopting the new process for our first batch of oxygen-blown steel. But JRD realized that opinion in Jamshedpur was divided, and the choice, so to speak, was finally thrust upon him. He called on his old friend, Dr Minoo Dastur of Dasturco, to confer with him. On that day, there was a cricket match going on. JRD told us, 'I'll get tickets for all of you to go to the cricket match, and I will decide along with Dr Minoo Dastur what is to be done.'

We were apprehensive but enjoyed the cricket match, and when we came back, he said, 'No, Jamshed, we will go by the more conventional process, the top-blown process. We will not take a risk with the OBM process.' I was personally disappointed but obviously, like a good soldier, had to accept the decision. We took one little precaution, though—we made the LD vessels with what is known as 'hollow trunnions' (the stands on which the vessel is placed), so that if we wanted to switch from top- to bottom-blown at a later date, we could do so easily. But that occasion never came, because the top-blown process proved to be an outright success.

Over time, the new OBM process was phased out. So JRD had taken absolutely the right decision, even though he was totally non-technical. Of course, we fully supported the engineering team, the metallurgical team and the works team. I was in charge for all of them, so to speak. That was our first oxygen-blown steel melting shop, and it was a great success.

Since that time, of course, we've set up several LD shops in Tata Steel.

Cold Rolling Mills and Golf Course
to the Rescue

With the incorporation of the new G blast furnace and other furnaces, the supply of good quality coke from the stamp-charged batteries and various other facilities, we had ensured that we were making good-quality hot-rolled steel. We now decided it was appropriate to move on to the next and probably the biggest step in our modernization programme, which was the installation of a cold rolling facility, to make cold-rolled steel.

We knew from our studies that the best cold rolling mills in the world at that time had been put up by the Japanese. They had all collaborated to establish the best cold rolling mills in the world over the past decade (maybe 8–10 in all). So, to get the technology in India, it was a natural decision to go to them first. We already had a good relationship with them, thanks to J.R.D. Tata's initial efforts with the Japanese companies, and we soon prepared a programme to visit one of them and their suppliers.

We formed a team of three persons to visit Japan—me, Mr Muthuraman, who would become my successor as managing director, and Niroop Mohanty. I was of the firm belief (like JRD) that you might put up the best equipment in the world, but unless you have good people to operate it, you would not meet with success. Niroop Mohanty was the person in charge of human resources in Jamshedpur, and we included him because we wanted to study the manpower requirements very closely.

We were treated extremely well by our Japanese hosts, who had lined up a series of visits for us—not only to the steel plants but also to the manufacturers of the equipment that went into the cold rolling mills. We had a thorough look at all aspects, discussed various issues with them and then had a final meeting in Tokyo. I thought, rather fondly, that it would be smooth sailing now, but it was not to be. To my surprise and disappointment, at that meeting in the boardroom, where there were about thirty Japanese executives, our plan to partner with the Japanese to bring the cold rolling mill technology to India was turned down.

Only the president of the Japanese firm spoke, as per their custom. All others remained quiet while the top boss addressed us. He told us that the technology we were looking at was a difficult one. What we had done up to that point with Tata Steel—the blast furnace, coke ovens, steel melting shops, continuous casters and so on—was very creditable, but a cold rolling mill was a different kettle of fish. They, in Japan, had perfected this technology after a decade of hard work, he said. He suggested that they were on good terms commercially and anything that India required in terms of cold-rolled strips, the Japanese would be ready to supply.

The message, in effect, was, 'Look, gentlemen, we think the cold rolling mill is beyond you. Anyway, when we are happy to continue to supply you with the best cold-rolled strips in the world, why do you want to go and set up your own cold rolling mills?' This was communicated to us in very good English by the president, with interpreters stepping in wherever necessary.

I listened to this rather polite lecture for about forty-five minutes, and then finally it was my turn to speak. I didn't give a long speech, but I made it clear that though we Indians may be behind the Japanese in technology, we had our national pride. We would make the cold-rolled strips ourselves. We were not going to rely on anybody for our requirements. We would make a success of our cold rolling mill. We had shown our prowess to them and others in the past decade by putting up facilities comparable to the best in the world, whether to purify iron making or produce good-quality steel and coke. We were now on our way to becoming the lowest-cost producer of steel in the world. We had already put up a bar and rod mill. So we would go ahead and put up a cold rolling mill as well, with or without the help of the Japanese. I think they took my words in good spirit.

I told my colleague S.L. Srivastava, chief of engineering and projects, that, in a way, we had been rebuffed there. But no matter, we had got others in the Western world. There were a host of other equipment manufacturers and technology providers. Soviet Russia was there, also among the best. So we sent messages to our engineers in Jamshedpur that Japan was 'out' and that we should scout for others.

We returned from Japan disappointed but not disheartened. If anything, we were more determined than before to make a success of a cold rolling mill. We went about our work full steam, contacting others with the same specifications we had prepared for the Japanese. Then, one day, about a month after our disappointing return from Japan, Srivastava came and told me that the Japanese had shown an inclination to re-enter the race! Because of problems with interpretation and language,

J.J. Irani in his childhood

At the convocation for his master's degree at
Sheffield, 1960

Cricket in Sheffield

Sheffield days

J.J. Irani with Daisy Irani at their
wedding, 1971

With Daisy Irani at home, 1983

J.J. Irani and Daisy Irani with
their children

Dr Irani, Daisy Irani and their children, 1991

With his boss Russi Mody

With V.G. Gopal, president of Tata Workers' Union

With Pope John Paul II, 1986

With Ratan Tata

Born on the same day, several years apart: With T.V. Narendran

With Ratan Tata at the inauguration of Hot Strip Mill, 1994

With a Japanese delegation

With Tata Steel employees

With J.R.D. Tata

At the convocation ceremony of XLRI, as chairman of the board of governors, 1998

At the convocation ceremony of IIM Lucknow, as chairman of the board of governors, 2009

Dr Irani delivered the 41st Hatfield Memorial Lecture at Sheffield University, 1993

With Mother Teresa, 1991

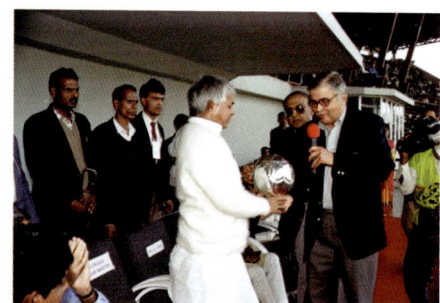

With Lalu Prasad Yadav

Receiving the Prime Minister Award for the best steel plant in India from former PM Atal Bihari Vajpayee

With former prime minister
P.V. Narasimha Rao

With former prime minister
Manmohan Singh

With former UK prime minister
John Major, 1993

With Prince Charles at the CII

With Queen Elizabeth II, 1997

Receiving the Padma Bhushan
from former President
A.P.J. Abdul Kalam, 2007

J.J. Irani and Daisy Irani
with their grandsons, 2019

they said, there seemed to have been some miscommunication. They had not intended to turn us down. All that, of course, was a load of rubbish, because we had understood each other perfectly and made our intentions very clear. They had not wanted to provide the cold rolling mill technology to us and instead wanted to keep supplying the finished product from Japan.

But since they were now showing an interest, we sent them the same papers we had already given to other manufacturers. We would not treat them differently. After a comparative study, we realized that the Japanese had given the best offer, both commercially and technically. They were by far the best, better than the Western manufacturers. So, though they had cost us roughly three months, we shook hands with them again. We did not go to Japan. This time, they came to India, and a few things were made clear to them.

It was decided that a Japanese firm, along with their equipment suppliers, would set up our cold rolling mill. The next question was how long it would take. When I asked them, they said they had recently set up a mill in Indonesia, near Jakarta, and that had taken them thirty-six months—from the ground digging to commissioning. I said, 'I'm not interested in what you did in Indonesia. What is your best performance in Japan? You claim that you have put up seven cold rolling mills in the past decade in Japan itself. So please tell us, how much time did it take you in Japan?'

They said that their latest mill, which had all the new features and improvements, was in Oita in south Japan, and it had taken them twenty-nine months to set it up. So, I said, 'Okay, we will do ours in twenty-eight.' Once again, they thought that we were talking through our hat, but the contract given to them was for twenty-eight months. We had already started with the ground clearance, and so the time schedule of twenty-eight months was adequate, I felt.

Later, I found out that they had actually made a programme for 33–34 months. But after the first year, with the ground clearances, foundations, etc., going ahead of schedule in Jamshedpur, the message from the Japanese teams in Jamshedpur to their principals in Japan was clear. They knew we meant business and were sticking to the schedule of twenty-eight months. Their colleagues in Japan, who needed to prepare training programmes, equipment and other advice, were asked to reschedule their deliveries to meet our expectations. So they became alert to our requirements. And our mill configuration was finalized. As I said earlier, the Japanese were quite taken aback by the speed with which we were operating.

Our golf course came to the rescue here. Once we had finalized the contract with the firm, I insisted that the training for our staff, who would operate and maintain the mill, be done in Jamshedpur and not in Japan. I wanted as many Indians as possible (who would be future operators of the mill) to be trained in India. Some may go to Japan, but the vast majority of them should be trained in India.

Once again, the president threw up his hands and said, 'But nobody wants to go to India to train your staff. We have found Jamshedpur on the atlas, and it's a small dot. Quite frankly, we don't know how we can induce so many of our people to go to India to train your people.'

So I said, 'You just send me a batch of seven or eight persons to start with and leave the rest to us.'

He agreed to that, and the seven or eight Japanese arrived in India. Now, the Japanese are avid golfers and very fond of the game, but because of space restrictions in Japan, and in particular in Tokyo, not many people can either plan for the space or afford the money to go and play golf. Along with showing them the site, we showed them the Beldih Golf Course, and we told them they could play golf there all day if they wanted, as long as they did their work. I said, 'You can start at sunrise, work during the day, and go back home and play golf again till sunset. The golf course is at your disposal.' They said, 'Oh, golf is a very expensive game in Japan. How will we pay for it?' I told them it would be totally free. They almost fell off their chairs.

That message went back to all their colleagues in Japan. And my friend, the president, said, 'Oh, I don't know what sort of magic wand you have waved, because now everyone wants to go to Jamshedpur!'

Another problem was food. The Japanese have very particular food habits, and they certainly would not eat our masala-laden Indian food. We have a great variety of food, from the tandoori in the north to the masala dosa in the south, but none that suits Japanese taste. So we took one of the hotels in Jamshedpur and told their management that they needed to convert the entire hotel, including the rooms, for our Japanese guests. We told them that when the Japanese started coming in, they would all stay at the hotel. The management also had to make arrangements to give them Japanese food. The hotel immediately agreed and got some chefs trained in Calcutta, and we were soon geared up to give Japanese food to our Japanese friends in Jamshedpur.

So both from the staying point of view and the food point of view, we had tied up the loose ends. The president, who had been worried about who would want to go to Jamshedpur, was now only worried about how to ration their stay in

Jamshedpur so that everyone could experience a little bit of the good life.

And that was how we solved the problem of bringing Japanese engineers to Jamshedpur!

What the Japanese Taught Us

From the Japanese connection, we learnt a lot more than how to emphasize on quality in our work. We learnt from them that in a group discussion only the 'leader speaks'! On the Japanese side, a leader's team members contribute only when he asks them to do so and fill in the gap. On the other hand, on the Indian side, there is a cacophony of voices; more than one person wants to talk at the same time, and sometimes the leader has to control them!

The Japanese always listen carefully; they are very polite, but also very firm. I don't know whether they prepare themselves beforehand regarding who will speak and so on, but as far as group discussions are concerned, there is no doubt left in the other party's mind about what they want to do and what they want to achieve. They convey their views and objectives precisely. They never interrupt each other. And they never contradict what their leader has said. Maybe they had closed-door discussions, but as far as their communication with us was concerned, it was crystal clear what they wanted to convey.

As I mentioned earlier, I was very keen that all the training for the project be done in Jamshedpur and, obviously, in English. The Japanese came to Jamshedpur and conveyed their views in English, on time and precisely. They would prepare all the documents regarding instructions, advice and so on in English, prior to our meetings, so that our team could read them and prepare for the discussions. The approach typified their thoroughness.

I remember one incident when one of our team members got up and said to the Japanese, 'Yes, we are very happy that you are giving us everything in writing. We are also very happy that you are answering all our doubts verbally. But tell me if, in spite of all these instructions and advice and documents, someone wants to transgress the advice which is given or does not follow the rules which have been laid down, what then? What would you do?'

The Japanese were amazed. They kept saying, 'But if everything is given in writing, everything is verbally explained, why should there be a need for any clarification?'

Our team member kept repeating his question: If, in spite of everything, somebody does not follow the rules, what happens?

This back-and-forth went on for about five minutes. And ultimately, I had to bring the matter to a close. The Japanese did not understand the question. It had never occurred to them that somebody would not follow the rules. Why should the rules not be followed? That, in my opinion, is the key difference between Japanese culture and our Indian culture. In India, we have a cacophony of voices, and in spite of clear instructions, people do tend to take 'shortcuts', sometimes with disastrous consequences.

Another thing I have noticed is that we Indians, when faced with an unusual situation, have the habit of settling the matter with what we call 'jugaad'. We make do with whatever is available, and somehow solve the problem and keep going. But the Japanese do not believe in jugaad. To them, everything must be in black and white, and is either right or wrong. There is no tolerance for ideas like 'make do with whatever is available'. And that is why, in my opinion, they are so well ahead in their technology and also in their attitudes towards making things work. The Indian attitude is to 'keep going somehow', with suboptimal solutions—as jugaad is acceptable—and carry on. Particularly, where safety is concerned, the Japanese will never deviate from the laid-down guidelines. When we first looked at the Japanese safety records in their plants, we were amazed at the consistency and high level of safety achieved in their operating plants. They are absolute fanatics when it comes to safety and will not accept the second best, will not deviate from the accepted levels of safety.

What was the most significant Japanese contribution? It was not on the technical side, not the various equipment they supplied, nor the various methods of operation they taught us. I believe their most important contribution was in teaching us the discipline to operate in a safe manner without taking any chances and without endangering the lives of our employees. For the Japanese this is a religion. Whatever has to be done must be done in a safe manner, or not done at all.

* * *

I would like to touch upon one or two subjects related to quality. In the 1960s and 1970s, Tata Steel lived through a system that did not encourage us to enhance the quality of our products. In fact, according to our topsy-turvy pricing system at that time, defective materials could be sold at a greater profit to the steel company than those which were certified under stringent quality codes. The reason was simple, though unfortunate. It was that the government controlled all the pricing of the tested grades of steel. The government at that time told steel companies what to make, how much to make of each grade, whom to sell to and at what price. Everything was controlled by a body called the Joint Plant Committee (JPC, Ministry of Steel). They laid down the price that, according to them, was fair. We were one of the only two private companies in the steel business. And for both companies the selling prices were laid down by the JPC.

Annual 'reviews' of the price were allowed to the producer. At that time, I was the chief metallurgist of Tata Steel. So it was my duty and my responsibility to go with my colleagues to Delhi and argue in the JPC why we should get a price increase. We did extensive studies in preparation—increase in the price of labour, increase in the price of infrastructure, railways freight, increase in the price of raw materials and so on—and then we would present a figure to the JPC. The chief at JPC would then arrive at a figure which everyone had to accept but with which no one was happy. Such was the government's will. Sometimes, in fact, we had to sell steel at a price lower than the manufacturing cost.

If there were 'defective' pieces, which did not conform to any of the laid-down quality standards, these could be sold in the open market. This was outside the purview of the JPC, and we could charge a price which the customer was prepared to pay. Traders would quickly gobble up these pieces and usually pay a price higher than that of steel of tested grades. Dealers were prepared to pay a higher price than the price of steel manufactured to specifications. We did not intentionally use 'defectives', but if the chief metallurgist of our company agreed that a certain batch of steel was 'defective' and did not conform to any of the specifications laid down, then it was taken out of our production schedule.

I think such a stance was totally against the quality movement. Because of the shortage in supply, customers were prepared to pay for defective material, which did not conform to any quality standards. The customers did not care if the steel did not meet a certain specification; they just wanted the material. It was a topsy-turvy attitude to quality, if I may say so.

Early Separation Scheme at Tata Steel: Modernizing the Mind

After the first three stages of modernization, during which we established a gleaning new blast furnace, coke oven batteries with a new stamp-charged technology, new LD shops and a number of new rolling mills, I was asked: What about phase four of modernization?

I realized that we were operating these new units with the same old mindset, and there was a need to modernize our minds. Though we had a very loyal and disciplined workforce, they needed a new orientation to operate successfully.

There was a joke at Tata Steel that if a father had three sons, he would educate the first as an engineer, the second as a doctor and the third he did not have to educate at all, because the father's job would pass on to the son as a matter of right. There was an understanding, in fact, a rule with the union that after serving the company for twenty-five years, a person could nominate anyone he wished for a permanent job in Tata Steel. Though we had a faithful and loyal workforce, this one-to-one replacement meant that we would never be able to reduce our numbers. And it became increasingly obvious that the workforce was bloated and needed to be reduced for our success in future years. We had a workforce of 80,000, and we just could not succeed in business with such large numbers. When Ratan Tata and I went abroad seeking funds for our various modernization programmes, we were continuously questioned not on our technology or on our ability to operate the steel plant, but on the very large number of workers; according to international standards, this was almost twice the number that was required.

We scripted an attractive voluntary retirement scheme (VRS) and offered it directly to the workers. It was so attractive that we did not have to pressure anyone into accepting that scheme. We set an annual target for the scheme. This target was reducing the workforce by 3000 or 4000 for some years, and by only a few hundred for others. In total, over a ten-year period, we reduced our workforce from 78,000 in 1992 to under 40,000 by the end of the 1990s. Approximately, 10,000 of these workers would have retired in normal course. But the remaining 30,000 were offered and accepted the VRS. I might also add that not one of those who took and opted for the scheme regretted it, because the terms were so generous, and the company had prepared the applicants for an alternative job outside Tata Steel. So those who took the scheme had the benefit of two sources of income. One was the Early Separation Scheme (ESS) benefit, and the other was the alternative job, which was eventually offered to them. It was said that work experience of a number of years in Tata Steel was itself a much sought-after qualification, and other employers were willing to pick up those who had opted out of Tata Steel as a result of our ESS scheme.

There are many related stories and experiences, some of which I would like to recount here. One thing this exercise taught me was how to talk to the workforce in a language they would understand. When I started on this ESS programme, there were many older workers who felt that I had robbed their sons or relatives of their jobs in Tata Steel. This was clearly expressed at some of our management–union meetings. To make my position understandable, I would tell the workers' unions and individual members that we were in an industrial intensive care unit (ICU). My plea to them was that as an industry, too, we are in an ICU, and there were two ways of getting out of ICU. The one and the better way was to undergo the pain of surgery and take some bitter medicines, get well and walk out of the ICU vertically, on your own feet. The other way was to say, no, I will not undergo painful surgery or swallow bitter medicines, and God will take care of me. Yes, without the surgery and medicines, God would take care of you, and you would move out of the ICU horizontally, on a stretcher, and be taken straight to the cremation grounds. Which way do you prefer to leave the ICU? And obviously, the answer dawned on them as they realized the situation we were in as an industry and why it was necessary to take painful decisions like reduction in jobs to get back to good health.

Those who were the first few to take the ESS benefits and move out on very attractive terms spread the message among their coworkers that it was not such a bad thing at all to leave Tata Steel and start a fresh career elsewhere. Once the workers understood the benefits of the scheme, we had no problems at all extending it year after year, over a period of ten years. In fact, even now, for short periods, this scheme is opened to a targeted set of workers, and they happily sign up for it.

Our scheme was so generous that some of my colleagues in the Confederation of Indian Industries (CII) and elsewhere told us that we either had too much money or too little brains. All I can say in our defence is that the administration of that scheme was so successful that it has found a place in a book titled *The Greatest Business Decisions of All Time*. It features case histories that revolutionized industry. Jack Welch and many other famous names are in that book, and there is only one case from India—the case of Tata Steel, which reduced its numbers dramatically over a period of ten years, ensuring that the company did not sink into bankruptcy as a result of having a grossly exaggerated workforce.

So my friends in the industry who thought that we either had too much money or too little brains, or a combination of the two, have been proved wrong. And Tata Steel has immensely benefited from the manpower reduction, because it is not just the salary that we save but also the associated facilities utilized by the workforce. The workers have to move out of their company-provided accommodation, with the result that it is no longer necessary to build more and more homes for our workforce. Also, though medical benefits continue, many of the workers who have taken the ESS scheme have moved out of Jamshedpur, so the load on our medical services has greatly reduced. There were many additional benefits of having a reduced workforce. People who took the ESS became its best ambassadors.

If I have to briefly comment upon the scheme as it stands now, I would say that the positive experience of the majority has encouraged many others to sign up for the scheme. No longer are they of the view that there is no world outside Tata Steel. There is, I insist, a very profitable world outside Tata Steel.

Funny Times in Jamshedpur

One rather amusing episode that I would like to narrate is related to a tree planted by Jawaharlal Nehru, when he came to Jamshedpur for the fiftieth-year celebration of the steel company in 1956. Prime Minister Nehru had planted the tree to inaugurate the Jubilee Park.

For the seventy-fifth anniversary of the steel company, which was in 1980–81, we wanted to plant some more trees. Someone said that it would be nice if we could tag those trees along with the tree planted by Nehru twenty-five years earlier. I was in charge of the steel plant by then, and I thought this was a very good idea. We decided that we would plant one tree to mark the seventy-fifth anniversary next to the tree that had been planted by Nehru for the fiftieth anniversary. It never occurred to me then that it would be difficult to trace that original tree planted by Nehru.

All those in service in 1995–96, and who were present at the Nehru ceremony, had retired. But quite a few of them had settled in Jamshedpur (such as Homi Bodhanwala, S.D. Sharma and many others). With them, we went to the park to identify 'the tree'. Over the twenty-five years that had elapsed since the fiftieth anniversary, several sturdy trees had grown up in the area, and there was no mark to pinpoint the tree planted by Nehru. All the old hands started arguing among themselves, pointing to different trees as the original one.

Finally, after about fifteen minutes of this rather aimless discussion, I told the party, 'Thank you, gentlemen, for your help. We shall identify the tree.' After they dispersed, I called Mr Karnad, who was the chief of the Parks and Gardens department, and, pointing to one nice, sturdy-looking tree, said, 'This is the tree!'

Of course, I had not even been present at the fiftieth-year ceremony! But when it was finally made known to all the others that the tree had been 'identified'—an identification I'd done just using my imagination—everyone concurred. 'Yes, this was the tree planted by Nehru, twenty-five years earlier.' We made a small platform around the tree—it is still there, commemorating that the tree was planted by Nehru in 1955–56, on the company's fiftieth anniversary! Of course, we now have a tree next to it— planted on the seventy-fifth anniversary. And after that, of course, another one to mark the hundredth anniversary too.

So, sometimes one has to use one's authority and position to end an impossible argument. This is an example of how at times, for a good cause, we have to deviate from the truth (because nobody really knows the truth). It is not such a bad thing, and if it is done with authority and clear-cut instructions, it is accepted by the community and audience! I would not advocate that this type of attitude should prevail in our normal, day-to-day life, that the man at the top 'dictates' what is the truth, but sometimes it is good to have what is known as a 'white lie' rather than allow the confusion to continue.

Sad Events and Tragedies in Jamshedpur

Every community has its joyous moments, which it celebrates, but also its sad ones. At Tata Steel, too, we have had our sad moments. We can only look back upon them with regret, with the community standing together as a means of consolation.

The worst tragedy that we suffered during my time in Jamshedpur was the fire on 3 March 1989, on Founder's Day. I would like to give some background. Almost from the day I joined Tata Steel, in January 1968, there had always been a lot of enthusiasm for celebrating Founder's Day, which falls every year on 3 March, the birthday of our founder, Jamsetji Tata. Every year, the whole company—spread not only across several locations in Bihar and now Jharkhand, but all over India—comes together to celebrate. Founder's Day is an occasion for the Tata family to get together every year and look forward to some sort of bonhomie. We don't get many occasions in the Tata Group to celebrate as a whole family, and so Founder's Day is the cause for a lot of joy and camaraderie.

I had noticed in 1968 itself how many divisions of the company would come together and talk very fondly of the celebrations on 3 March. The fervour for Founder's Day kept increasing through the 1970s and 1980s. The company supported this event financially, and all individuals and different locations came forward, to make sure that every nook and corner of the company felt the impact of Founder's Day get-togethers. J.R.D. Tata used to attend all of them, as did Russi Mody and the other directors.

At the centre of the celebrations was the grand parade, which was held at the main gate of the steel company in Jamshedpur. I think through the 1970s and 1980s, we might have made a mistake in introducing a strong, competitive spirit in this regard. We started offering prizes and other incentives to induce people to participate. So rather than just celebrating, the different divisions tried to outdo each other to get the attention of the management. And the homage to the founder, in a way, took second place as compared to our enthusiasm to vie with each other and win prizes. Throughout the 1980s, the morning parade grew in stature, and the spectators grew in number. From simple seating arrangements, we started building multilevel pandals, and everyone would try to get passes and tickets for seats as close as possible to the founder's bust, which was, of course, the centrepiece of the whole event.

Every year, there were more and more people attending, both from within Tata Steel and guests. People wanted to be seen with the VIPs, shake hands, be photographed and so on. The closer you were to the founder's bust, the closer you were to the VIPs, who would move around freely, shaking hands and rubbing shoulders with the junior officers, their wives and their families. The parade also became grander and longer. We would start at 7 a.m. and finish around 11 a.m.

In 1989, we had reached a peak. That was one year when J.R.D. Tata and Ratan Tata were not with us for the celebrations. We started off with the parade as usual, and once again, there was a lot of jostling and pushing to be seen. Women and children were also present in large numbers. Unfortunately, at around 10.30

a.m., when the procession from the Tata Steel's subsidiary TCIL was coming into view, a firework landed on top of the multilevel pandal that had been constructed in that area. It immediately caught fire, and within five minutes there was a raging inferno. Though safety exits had been provided, the passages got congested, and the net result was that within ten minutes of our noticing the fire on the roof of the pandal, people were trapped.

K.C. Mehra, the deputy managing director, I and another colleague tried to pull as many out of the inferno as we could, but twenty people died on the day. By the end of the week, the figure went up to forty, and by the time that the whole matter was settled and the last of the injured were taken care of, the death toll was exactly sixty. It was a great blot on the festivities.

For the next one month, my time and Daisy's was divided between visiting the injured who were recovering at the TMH and paying visits to those families which had suffered losses; and, of course, during the first few days, in visiting the pyres of the dead on the banks of the Subarnarekha River. It was a very grim, very tragic moment for all of us.

I distinctly remember one case of an officer who is still with us. His son had suffered burns. I used to visit the lad twice a day in the hospital. He was only about ten or twelve years old at the time. After about 8–10 days, he suddenly developed a liking for hamburgers. There was no McDonald's or anything like that in Jamshedpur at that time, but I arranged with a kitchen to serve this particular dish to the youngsters—not only to him but also to the others who wanted it. I visited him one morning when he was eating a hamburger. He seemed quite happy. I congratulated him and felt relieved that at least in this difficult time, we were able to give him some food that he liked. Unfortunately, one evening when I went to visit him, the doctor sadly told me that he was no more. He had developed some lung problems, and

though he had had a breakfast of hamburgers, he was on the
funeral pyre by that same night. So, like that, there were many
personal cases of tragedy, too numerous to be enumerated
here. One family I remember suffered three deaths, during or
after the fire. And there were many with multiple casualties.
Children of some senior officers had also been injured at the
fire and later expired.

JRD was in Geneva at the time of the incident. He and Ratan
Tata flew down to Jamshedpur immediately on hearing of the
tragedy and were with us on the morning of 5 March, less than
two days after the event. JRD made it a point to visit each and
every family that had suffered a loss. He kept on telling us not
to be stingy or hold back on whatever was required to help the
injured, and, above all, to make sure that the company stood by
its obligations and went above and beyond what was required.
We did whatever could be done in India. But we also sent some
of them to places like Paris and London, so that their wounds
could be properly treated. We wanted to do our best to reduce the
pain and the suffering of the injured and bereaved. The Tatas and
our management made sure that money was not a consideration.
We did not, in any way, hold back on matters of health due to
financial considerations.

I would like to recall one episode in relation to this. Summer
was fast approaching in March, and at that time we had no special
ward for burn victims. Realizing that the summer heat would
only increase the pain of the injured, I urged the air-conditioning
experts of Voltas to put in all efforts required to turn one floor
of the JGMH, our main hospital, into an air-conditioned unit.
Voltas rose to the challenge, picked up air conditioners from
wherever they could in Jamshedpur, and within forty-eight hours
we had air-conditioned the entire floor. We could house about
sixty patients in the air-conditioned space.

I remember particularly the advice and help that I received at that time from one of our directors, L.P. Singh, who was the former secretary and chief secretary of the Bihar government, and later became the home secretary of the Government of India in Delhi. He was in Delhi at that time. And as he had experience of such events, I relied on his inputs heavily. He had predicted that we would suffer in the first week. Naturally, the bereaved families would say 'Why us?' and we would have to go out of our way to convince them that we were doing everything possible to help the injured and bereaved. So, as L.P. Singh had predicted, the first week was full of anger. People were asking us why they had lost their dear ones and why they were suffering. After that, when they realized that the company was going all out to redress whatever injuries and grievances there were in the Tata Steel family, they would be grateful for some time. Not even the government would have given them such succour in such a short span of time. This phase of gratitude would last for about a month. And then, some people, particularly those who were not directly involved with the tragedy, would start thinking about how they could benefit from the tragedy.

Everything happened exactly as L.P. Singh had told me. The first week was indignation, followed by a month of gratitude and realization that the company was trying to help. And then some folks came to explore how best they could extract money from the company. In this last they were not very successful, because right from the beginning we had worked on our employees and their families, to ensure the best help for them in this difficult hour.

Even now, every year on 3 March we have a two-minute silence near the founder's statue, in memory of those who died. This is by far the most tragic event in my living memory, as far as Tata Steel is concerned.

* * *

There were some other tragedies too, and I will briefly touch upon them. As everyone knows, we have an aviation department, and thanks largely to J.R.D. Tata and later to Ratan Tata, this department has always been kept well supplied and funded for buying planes, which are required in the course of our operations. Tata Steel has many units—iron mines, manganese mines, coal mines—spread over a vicinity of, say, 50–150 miles from Jamshedpur. That was the vision of the founders when they established the company in Jamshedpur—they wanted raw materials to be fetched from nearby Jamshedpur and turned into steel. Though there were roads to reach these places, for senior executives, precious time was lost in traversing the terrain. At times one had to drive 5–6 hours from those locations to reach Jamshedpur. So, the company very wisely invested in some small planes and kept an active aviation department to fetch at least the senior executives quickly from these locations to Jamshedpur. We have had this facility for maybe forty years.

In the 1970s, we had a very active pilot, Captain V.P. Agrawal. He was not someone who would take unnecessary risks. One cloudy morning, he had to fly to Jamadoba. On cloudy days, the peaks around Jamshedpur also get covered. That morning, there was a commercial flight from Calcutta. When Captain Agarwal came to the control room and saw the conditions, he advised the pilot of the incoming flight to turn back. He said, 'Visibility is not good, so please don't take the risk and go back to Calcutta.' The pilot did that. But half an hour later, Captain Agrawal himself took off in one of our small four-seater planes to go to Jamadoba to pick up a passenger from there—against his own advice, because he was so confident, I suppose.

The Dalma hills surround Jamshedpur in the north. A valley is formed between two of the hills, less than 3000 feet in height. All a pilot had to do was to circle around the Jamshedpur airport till the plane reached an altitude of 3000 feet, and then fly away in whichever direction he wished to, because at above 3000 feet, the plane would be clear of all obstructions. But for some reason, on that morning, Captain Agrawal decided to fly through the valley. And very sadly, he had miscalculated and hit the southern peak just outside Jamshedpur. It was a great tragedy. It took us several hours to find the wreckage.

So that was another incident where the whole community was saddened. His wife was immediately given employment at Tata Steel, but, of course, no amount of help could bring back the deceased member of the family. I still remember JRD, who was in Bombay when he was informed of the incident. By mid-morning, he phoned me and kept on asking why he didn't circle over Jamshedpur to 3000-plus feet and then head towards his destination. I was obviously not in a position to give him the answer. But to JRD, an experienced pilot himself, it was beyond comprehension that someone would take such a risk. That day, we lost a good friend and a good pilot.

* * *

Twice during my time, we witnessed communal riots. These usually started with a very minor incident, and then the lumpen elements in the community took the initiative of pitting one religion against another. During the second of these riots, I had reached a position of seniority. It was in 1978, I think, and it was tragic to see how the *goondas* and the riffraff had taken charge of the city. There was mayhem for two to three days. After peace was restored, the military officer (Jamshedpur is home to a military unit, as it is used as a staging post from India to the Far East) in charge told me that the situation had been like a full-scale military operation. The goondas of one community living to the north of the Subarnarekha had to be literally fought out, gunned out; they had collected so much arms and ammunition that a military operation had to be mounted to quell that situation.

Nobody knows how many died. The unofficial figure is somewhere between 300 to 400. It was very sad to see people who had lived together suddenly positioning themselves at opposite ends of a fight. I remember one particular instance during the last riot. We were using our hospital ambulance, to evacuate those who had been entrapped and encircled. We had made several trips to bring out the women and children when the goondas came to know that we were using the ambulance. So the next time the ambulance visited that area, they locked the doors of the vehicle from outside, poured petrol on it and incinerated the whole lot. About twenty innocent died. It was very tragic.

Such events had one lasting effect on Jamshedpur that I have myself noticed. On occasions when I offered good accommodation facilities to members of the minority community, they would turn down that offer. When asked why, they would answer that they had already experienced communal violence twice in their life, and that they felt safe only when residing in their own neighbourhoods, with their families and community.

Of course, Jamshedpur always managed to emerge from such tragedies with goodwill. But it was sad that such events transpired at all, not once but twice in my lifetime. So I can sympathize with those who would prefer to live surrounded by members of their own community. Even now, Jamshedpur has certain areas which are well known and earmarked as 'minority areas'. And we just cannot break these up, because of reservations expressed by the members of these communities. We can sympathize with those who want to live together in their own way. They wish to do this for the protection of their families and not for any other ulterior motives.

It has been more than forty years since the last such incident in Jamshedpur, and I do hope that we are not faced with a similar situation in the future.

Part III

ALLIANCES, ENCOUNTERS
AND REFLECTIONS

On Caste

I strongly oppose and, in fact, abhor the caste-wise division of our country. It is extremely unfair to sections of our society that they are disadvantaged just because they do not belong to the 'right' caste, which is determined at their birth.

I would like to elaborate that there is a faint caste-wise distinction among the Zoroastrians and the Parsis too. But it has no influence on day-to-day activities, and the priestly caste does not in any way try to impose sanctions on those who do not belong to that caste. Both my sons-in-law are from priestly families, but I am not, and there has been no disadvantage to my daughters on this score. I recall that during one of our public meetings on affirmative action, when I was on the stage, someone from the audience challenged me by questioning whether I would give the hand of one of my daughters, or of both my daughters, to a low-caste person. My answer was immediate and from the heart: who my daughters decide to marry is not to be adjudicated by me; it is entirely a matter of their choice. As long as he is an honest and decent human being, I have no objection to my daughters marrying whoever they have chosen as life partner. I am happy that it has turned out to be exactly so for both my daughters.

I was fortunate that I was in a position to do away with caste identification at the time of my employment in Tata Steel. The employment procedure at Tata Steel, and also at other Tata companies, takes no cognizance of the caste factor, and I gave it not the slightest importance in my workday or social decisions. I have found great friendship and support from those whom I have embraced and who have appreciated my strict neutrality, as far as decision-making is concerned, on the issue of caste. It is an unfortunate facet of Indian society that even people in high places, who should know better, even now get influenced in their decision-making on the basis of caste. And as a result, the so-called lower-caste people continue to suffer an injustice, which they certainly do not deserve.

Mitigating National Problems
with J.R.D. Tata

Population Control

JRD was very ardent about and supportive of the family-planning programme. This was the 1970s, and to him there was nothing more important than inspiring people to reduce the size of their family and keep it to a maximum of two children. When he came to Jamshedpur, he would always expound on this and ask us what we were doing on this front.

We had started a programme for men, under which whoever got a vasectomy would receive an incentive of Rs 200. When I told him this, JRD exploded, saying, 'Only two hundred rupees?' (Mind you, in the mid-1970s, Rs 200 was worth quite a bit.) He said, 'Jamshed, this is more important than any of the blast furnaces and rolling mills that you are planning and want me to finance. This is far more important to the country. You don't only have to think about the company. You must think about the country.' He told me to increase the incentive amount, which was the same for everybody (not just for Tata Steel employees), to Rs 2000 per head.

I protested, saying such an increase would render us broke. Eventually, after discussions with my colleagues, we agreed to increase the amount from Rs 200 to Rs 400 for any person—male or female—signing up for the programme.

Drinking Water

Today, Jamshedpur has 100 per cent pure water supplied through our system, but at one time it did not, and drinking water was a problem. JRD was very keen that we supply good clean water not only to our colonies but to the whole of Jamshedpur. One thing he always insisted upon was that if we did anything like this, it should be for the whole town and not just for the Tata portion of the population, which was at that time less than 30 per cent of the town's population.

When he asked me what we were doing about the issue, I took him to our new water purification plant, which was on the banks of the Kharkai River. I used to drive him around, so as we got out of the car, a bearer came up with two glasses of water.

JRD said, 'I'm not feeling thirsty.'

But I told him, 'No, this is the custom in this part of India. If you visit someone, they will always serve you water. If you don't drink it, the person offering the water might be offended.'

So, very gingerly, he took the glass and took a few sips. After he had swallowed, I told him that the water he had just drunk had been purified from our sewage system, and he exploded. He said, 'What? Jamshed, you made me drink that?'

I replied, 'Yes, I have also drunk it, and you can see its taste is normal. It is perfectly healthy.'

I don't think he liked the idea very much. He became quiet, and I spent our return journey wondering whether I still had my job. But then JRD realized the importance of doing something different, and we were back to normal.

Statues

Another thing JRD ardently opposed was statues. All towns in India, even small villages, have statues of Mahatma Gandhi, and, in some cases, of other local heroes too. When I came to Jamshedpur, I was surprised—there were no statues. There was only one bust of the founder, J.N. Tata, and another bust of P.N. Bose, who had helped in locating the steel plant in Sakchi and had found the iron ore deposits of Mayurbhanj. The chief geologist of the Mayurbhanj royal family, he had convinced Jamsetji Tata that we had enough iron resources in this part of the world to set up a steel plant, a fact that was confirmed later by geologist C.M. Wells. Together they had located the iron ore deposits in Gurumasani.

In Jamshedpur, there were no statues even of Jamsetji's son, Sir Dorab Tata, who was the first chairman of the company and had implemented his father's vision. Jamsetji Tata was a visionary. He dreamt, he wrote letters to his son that laid out in minute detail what Jamshedpur should look like: hockey and football fields, mandirs and temples, gardens and wide streets with flowering trees.

Jamsetji paid great attention to detail. There were no planes then, and voyages to Europe and America took three to four weeks. He utilized that time on the ship to think and to write to his son what should be done in the steel city. But all this was in the mind's eye of the founder. He didn't live to see any of it; it was his son who faithfully implemented his father's wishes in what is Jamshedpur now.

We now have busts of JRD in Jamshedpur. And the local population, particularly the Adivasis, have put up statues and busts of their leaders. But the steel company has never encouraged anyone to put up statues. In fact, I cannot recall statues of any worthies in Jamshedpur. We have not put up any statues. We have one of Sir Dorab Tata in the Dorab Tata Park, and a JRD bust in the new JRD stadium. In fact, when we put up a bust of JRD in the new stadium—we call it the J.R.D. Tata stadium—he couldn't say no because we had already done it, but I don't think he was overly pleased to see himself in the marble bust form.

Knighthood and Forging Indo–British Partnership

As far as my interactions with eminent people are concerned, I will start with Queen Elizabeth II. I had grown up during the days of the British Raj, and my parents were quite unabashed, keen supporters of the royal family. In fact, I recall that in my bedroom, photographs of two princesses—Princess Margaret and Princess Elizabeth—stared down on me. Some admiration!

I became the president of CII in 1991 and had to interact with many eminent personalities. Queen Elizabeth comes first to my mind. She visited India in 1997, and I met her in Delhi as well as in Bombay. By that time, I had done quite a lot of work for Indo–British partnership, and this had led to my getting a recognition from the British government in the form of an honorary knighthood (KBE: Knight of the British Empire). Technically, this made me a 'Sir', though I could not use the title because India was independent by that time and my knighthood was an honorary one.

I would like to add a little bit here about the work I did for Indo–British partnership. I led the Indian end of this initiative for five years since its inception. At that juncture, the industries of England and India had to be brought together. I told my colleagues in India and my compatriots on the British side that the Indo–British partnership programme should act like a marriage bureau. We should bring appropriate partners from either side together, introduce them, facilitate their interaction and then leave it to the individual companies on both sides to work out a marriage. If it happened, fine; if it didn't happen, we could not enforce it. But the mere act of bringing the companies together would naturally promote some sort of bonhomie, and out of that a useful result would be produced.

The whole idea of the partnership, by the way, was mooted by me when John Major, the then prime minister of the UK, visited India sometime in the early 1990s. I was president of the CII, and knowing his interest in cricket, I used a cricketing analogy in my introductory speech. I pointed out that the UK, with the US, was in the opening partnership of a cricket team, when independence was granted to India. But since then, maybe out of neglect or indifference from both sides, they had fallen in the rankings. They had begun batting in the middle order—number five or six—because the USSR, Japan and even Canada had overtaken the UK.

The fault was on both sides. British industries considered India a place where they could not do business easily, due to too many regulations, too many restrictions, too much interference from the government. The Indian view was that British engineering and technology were already secondary to those available in the US and maybe in many other countries. So we were not interested. If they didn't want a partnership, we didn't want a partnership. This had resulted in a downgrading of industry relationships between the two countries. I said that unless we do something about this, the UK will be dropped out of the team altogether.

John Major's response to this speech was very positive. He told me that it was his intention to bring England up in the batting order once again. And that we industrialists must suggest the best, the most convenient way in which Indian and British industries could come together and forge partnerships.

That was the birth of Indo–British partnership in 1991. As the CII president, I was, in a way, the natural choice to lead this initiative from the Indian side. Another suitable person, the chairman of British Oxygen, was chosen to lead the initiative from the British side, and both of us were told to select our teams from our respective industries. We met in London, Delhi, Bombay and Edinburgh over the next few years, forging many partnerships. The Indian prime minister at that time was Narasimha Rao. Although a man of few words, he was a very sagacious person. He understood the importance of what we were doing and always gave us the necessary encouragement through his officers.

So for five years after 1991, it was a very busy period for our respective industries. And after five years, my term was over. But by that time Indo–British partnership had been very successfully and firmly forged. I think I was given the honorary title in recognition of this.

Normally, these titles are given at Buckingham Palace, on the queen's birthday, sometimes to several hundred people at the same time. But that was not the case with me. Obviously, I could not go to London just for that one evening, and since the queen was coming to India that same year, 1997, it was decided that I would have a single separate investiture. My title investiture ceremony was held at the British high commission in Delhi on 14 October 1997. Unfortunately, we were told not to carry any cameras; the queen's protocol did not allow photos. But we could take four guests. I took Daisy, my two daughters and another family friend, all ladies, to the ceremony.

The queen was very gracious during the ceremony. I was given a certificate. When I mentioned to her that there was no indication of her presence on the certificate, which was signed by Prince Philip, she took out a pen and signed the certificate. I have proudly displayed it in my study.

So that was five years spent with the Indo–British partnership initiative, which is still thriving. Every five years, there is a change in leadership on both sides.

Building an Alliance with
Lalu Prasad Yadav

Lalu Prasad Yadav, the former chief minister of Bihar, was a student leader who came into prominence in the late 1980s. He must have been about thirty at that time, and he rose very fast from being a student leader to the chief ministership. We both came to our peak at the same time—in about the same duration, I rose in the Tata organization to become the chief executive officer and managing director of Tata Steel.

I decided that we should take some steps to orient him in the right direction in terms of what the Tatas are and what the Tatas can do for Bihar. But since it was a political matter, I thought it best to first approach my board in Bombay, inform them about what was happening and take their inputs on whether we should come to an understanding with him. One or two of the very senior members did not understand why I wanted to indulge a politician. They were of the view that chief ministers didn't last long in Bihar. Statistics showed that because of the political instability in the 1980s, a CM lasted for less than a year.

But I thought that this student leader was going to be more prominent than the past chief ministers and believed we should try to make peace with him or at least make him understand our way of life. So I was given permission to go and talk to Lalu Prasad Yadav. In hindsight, this was just as well, because Lalu Prasad and his wife, Rabri Devi, ruled Bihar for fifteen years.

So I sought a meeting with him. Lalu readily agreed. I went to Patna and spent one morning with him. His English was much worse than my Hindi, so we carried out the conversation in Hindi. When I entered his room, around 15–20 people were there. But everyone was sent packing with one imperious wave of his hand, and only he and I were left. I started off in my broken Hindi about the Tatas' long history of operating in Bihar. By 1980, we had worked in Bihar for almost eighty years. I told him he must come and see what we had done (he had never been to Jamshedpur). I said we would like to do something similar in other parts of Bihar and, of course, improve our own standing in Jamshedpur. I told him, quite frankly, that the Tatas had been in Bihar for over eighty years and would continue in the state long after both he and I had exited the scene.

I could make out that he was listening intently to me. Every time I made a point, his favourite comment was, ' *Theek hai* [All right]!' I went on to explain to him that we could not give monies to political parties but that we had a lot of money for social projects that benefited society and the people. If the state wanted to build a school or a hospital, or repair a bridge during times of flood, or provide food during famine, we had plenty of money. We didn't want to claim credit for doing the good work. It would all be done in their name, according to their wishes. Once again, he said, 'Theek hai.' And after about an hour of this conversation, he once again waved his hand imperiously. The interview was over. I came away from the meeting not sure what the impact had been. But as an aside I can tell you that from that moment till now, almost thirty years later, he has never made an improper request of us, whether me personally or the Tatas in general. His general attitude has been, 'Tatas are my friends. They are welcome to work in Bihar. We should give them all the facilities to continue with their programmes.'

Lalu Prasad took me up on my offer to visit Jamshedpur. I showed him around the steel plant. He was not interested in blast furnaces and steel melting shops and rolling mills. But what caught his eye were the trackscavators (earth-moving equipment) we had imported from the USA and which were used for clearing slag and bricks in our waste-material yards. He told me that he needed this equipment to clean up areas at the Patna railway station and other vital points in Patna, where there were, apparently, piles and piles of rubbish and garbage.

So I said, 'Okay, we will give these to you, on one condition. We will supply you with the drivers, fuel, mechanics to keep them going. But you must send all those people back in two weeks.'

He said, 'Theek hai.'

When I told our maintenance people, they said, 'Oh, God. Boss, what have you done? We will never get this equipment back. Let's find a way to avoid giving the equipment, because they are all imported and difficult to procure.'

I said, 'No, I've given my word, they will go.'

And we sent them off to Patna. Lalu himself supervised to see how the cleaning was done. Those trackscavators were made to work around the clock by our crew, and they cleaned up the areas he had in mind. In exactly two weeks on the dot, he put them back on those trailers, and everything and everyone returned to Jamshedpur—much to the amazement of our engineers and officers, who had thought that we had lost them forever.

During that time, there was an interesting episode. It was wintertime and around eleven o'clock at night. We were having a party at a hotel in Patna when one of my colleagues came and told me that the chief minister was here, and that the durban of the hotel wasn't letting him in because the CM had come incognito. I immediately rushed out to be greeted by an amazing sight. Lalu Prasad had a shawl around his shoulder, and was wearing a woolen cap and a big thick scarf, as it was wintertime. I don't blame the durban; nobody could have recognized him as the chief minister of Bihar. And so he was stopped at the entrance to the hotel. I apologized and brought him in. He didn't drink anything, but we had a good chat, and he was very happy with that. So that was one of the steps which we took to build bridges with him. He was proud of his relationship with the Tatas and did everything possible to help us.

Soon after my first visit to his office, I was told that the Patna Medical Hospital was in the pits. It had very poor quality of service, hygiene and so on. But they were short of one particular service: childcare. There was no hospital for children. I said, 'Okay, we will build an entire block only for children from our funds.' The only condition was that we would be totally in charge of building it and, also, later of running it—we would put our doctors, train their doctors and supply the medicines. We would look after hygiene. Everything would be done as if it was a part of the Tata Main Hospital (TMH) in Jamshedpur. Once again, Lalu agreed. We ran the hospital as we ran the TMH, and it became the talk of the town in Patna—how clean it was, how efficient and how smoothly people were taken care of.

Lalu Prasad greatly appreciated this, and it established us as an organization that desired to help the people of Patna. It added to our credibility, the most important factor in gaining recognition in any community. People must believe that you will do tomorrow what you are talking about today, that you don't make wild promises but promises you can keep.

Another thing Lalu wanted, naturally, was that we set up industrial facilities in Jamshedpur. At that time, we were in talks about the hot strip mill. In fact, we had already taken a decision to set it up in Orissa. According to Orissa's industrial policy, if a project cost more than Rs 500 crore, which in the early 1990s was an astronomical figure, the Orissa government would give some tax benefits. There was no such provision in the Bihar Factory Act or statutes. So I explained to Lalu that Orissa was giving these benefits, which was why we were going there. He turned around and asked, 'How quickly do you need this provision?' Usually, this kind of statute change takes years. I told him that we needed it within 2–3 months. He said, 'All right, I will look into it. Don't go to Orissa and don't sign anything.' And in record time, the factory acts statutes of Bihar were changed.

Naturally, we then had no excuse to go to Orissa. We decided to put up the mill in Jamshedpur, and it is still running beautifully. So in a way, Lalu saved that money going out of Bihar and into Orissa. Of course, since then, we have invested much, much more in Jamshedpur and elsewhere in Bihar. The point I'm making here is that Lalu had the capacity and the driving force to get such things done if he wanted to. He could move the assembly and his legislators.

I remember another incident related to this. Once he had made that change and we had finalized plans to establish the mill on the ground, we required certain facilities and certain sanctions for our plans to be put into action. A few weeks later, S.L. Srivastava, our general manager of engineering, came and told me, 'Look, we have got all the drawings ready, but these drawings have to be signed by the factory inspector to allow us to do this work.' The factory inspector had already delayed the matter by three weeks by not signing those papers.

Just then, Lalu visited Jamshedpur and stayed at the circuit house. I, along with Arun Narayan Singh, who knew Bihar's background, went there to meet him. He once again cleared the room, and I told him of our problems. I said that one person was holding up the process, and if that man was expecting something, we would never give him anything. Lalu heard me out and then said, '*Haan* [Yes]!' He told his durban in Hindi, '*Usko bulao* [Call him].'

When the chief minister was in town, all government officials were present in the same building, hovering around. Within minutes, the poor fellow came in meekly, hands folded, into the room. There was an empty chair around where we were sitting, and I gestured to him to sit down. But Lalu said no; he made a gesture suggesting that the man should remain standing. So this poor fellow, with his hands folded in front, stood before us. And then, for the next five minutes, Lalu gave him a dressing-down in the crudest of terms and in a loud of voice. (I didn't understand most of what he said, because he was speaking in Bhojpuri, and I don't understand Bhojpuri, though Arun Narayan Singh did.) The man left the room in a sweat. He signed the necessary papers in the next twenty minutes. But I told Lalu that this was not the way to behave with his subordinates. He could have scolded him separately, not in front of us. I was quite harsh with him, actually.

I dislike people who try to throw their weight around because of their position in an organization. To me, position and power are to be exercised with restraint and in office, not out in public. When I have to rebuke somebody, I have always made it a point to do it in private, never in front of anyone else. I have also taken pains to bring up my children with the same attitude.

Nothing has pleased me more as regards my two girls than when the principal of their school remarked that the Irani sisters had no airs and behaved just like any other girls, and never, in any way, threw their weight around using their parents' position in the company and in the town. This, to me, is more important than scoring high grades in school examinations.

I would like to recount an incident to drive home my point. In Tata Steel at one time, we used to have medical examinations for officers over a two-day period, and the intervening night was spent in a hospital cabin. On one such occasion, during the intervening night, dinner was called. When the gong was struck to announce that the food would be distributed, all of us took a tray and queued up in front of the wagon which brought the food. Most of us were in our kurta pajamas. There was no distinction between who was senior and junior. Just before the distribution of food began, one of the cabinet doors opened and a reasonably senior officer, but certainly not of my rank and of many others who were present, burst out of his room, grabbed the tray and demanded from the attendant that he be served food first because he was a senior officer! People who had seen me in the queue started to giggle, and the poor server was in a quandary. The person who had pushed himself to the head of the queue could not understand why the server had not started dishing out food to him first. When the poor server and attendant continued to hesitate, having seen that several other senior officers and I were already in the queue, the offended gentleman looked around. He saw me way down in the queue waiting for my turn and just dropped his tray and bolted back into his cabin, much to the amusement of all his colleagues who had gathered for dinner. This exemplifies the type of attitude I have thoroughly discouraged and disliked.

All of us are equal on the social front. And no one should try to throw their weight around because of their seniority in common spaces. I have tried my best to imbue this spirit in my family and also in the organization. And I think it has been appreciated. Seniority is okay in office and at meetings, where decisions may have to be taken, but it has no place in civil society.

So I told Lalu that he should learn this from me. I don't know whether he learnt it or not, but I've always believed that you if you have to reprimand a person, do it in private, never in front of anybody else. All men have dignity, and we have to recognize that dignity.

* * *

I don't think Lalu would be hurt if I say that there was no commonality between his and our way of administrating, excepting that in some areas we saw the same benefits. I always used to say that if you give Lalu a finger, he may yank off your arm; but if you don't give him that finger, he will see your point of view and we'll both be able to shake hands and count the fingers on each hand. So don't give in to what you might think is a small favour. If that small favor is not according to your ethical standards and rules, it is disastrous to extend it. It may look small, but ultimately it might throw up something totally unacceptable. So, stick to your principles.

Even in the most diverse cases, there are always areas, small areas, where there is commonality. And the job of the skilful negotiator on both sides is to earmark those areas of commonality.

Even if it's a very small percentage of the total sphere— 2 per cent, 5 per cent, 10 per cent, whatever—we should focus on those areas of commonality and come to agreements where both of us are on the same page. And then, having earned the confidence of each other, try to expand from there. The most important thing is that we should find out that narrow common space. It is like putting your foot through the door, and then slowly pushing yourself in. We don't have to ask the other party to sacrifice any of their principles; we don't have to sacrifice our principles. But those small areas where our principles meet, we should expand on them.

This is a management principle I have followed. Always seek small areas where you can agree with the other side without in any way sacrificing on ethics. That's the point where you can start and then build up confidence.

Here is one example of how we built a steady alliance. Once, there was a natural disaster, and a call came from Patna to rush some relief supplies. I don't know if it came from the chief minister or someone else. But a lot of blankets were required. There was nobody to help the people, and there was no time. Overnight, we had to send 200–300 blankets from our hospital. I always used to tell Lalu that we didn't want our name on whatever we gave, not because we were embarrassed but because we wanted him to take the credit. 'You should not think of this as being given by Tatas.'

I've built up that confidence further even after he left the chief ministership. When for a short period he was the railways minister in Delhi, I was approached by one of the Tata companies. They had heard that I had a good relationship with Lalu. So they came to me and told me that in regard to some tender quotation in the railways, they felt they were being treated unfairly. Could I intervene? It had nothing to do with my business, but I thought I could help them. So I went and met Lalu in Delhi.

He immediately pressed a button, and the durban came in. The chairman of the Railway Board was sitting in the next room. Lalu said, 'Unko bulao.'

After two minutes the durban came back and said, '*Wo saheb meeting chair kar rahe hain* [He is chairing a meeting].'

Lalu replied, '*Hamne bola, unko abhi bulao* [I said, call him now].'

The poor chairman of the Railway Board came with hands folded, looking very sheepish. Lalu just said, '*Ye hamara dost hain, yeh Tata wala hain, jo kuch chahata hai kar do* [He is my friend, from Tata. Do whatever he wants you to do].'

I remember a trip we took together to Singapore. On the plane, Lalu was, as usual, chewing tobacco (khaini) and paan, and spitting into a spittoon. I was sitting across the aisle from him, on the front seat. He kept spitting. I told his secretary, '*Aap mukyamantri ko bataiye* [tell the chief minister], if he spits in Singapore and they catch him, they will fine him fifty dollars the first time. They don't care who it is. The second time he's caught, he'll be put behind bars for one day. So please tell him to refrain from eating paan and spitting while we're in Singapore.'

The secretary must have conveyed the message. We were in Singapore for three days, and I never once saw him chew paan. He had that kind of discipline.

On the first day in Singapore, we had a meeting with a minister. It was a disaster. Lalu tried to speak in English, but I could sense that the minister couldn't get much of what he said. During the tea break, I approached Lalu, took him into a corner and said, 'Look, when the French minister comes to Delhi, he speaks in French. When the German chancellor comes to Delhi, he speaks in German. There are interpreters. When you are in Singapore, you speak in Hindi, and I will be your interpreter.'

'Theek hai.' He agreed.

After that he performed very well. Though he never saw the prime minister, he met many ministers, and they must have conveyed their impressions to the Singaporean prime minister.

When the Singaporean PM met Ratan Tata 2–3 weeks after our visit, he told Mr Tata that his ministers had been most impressed by the chief minister of Bihar. That was how Lalu could influence and impress people.

Encounters with Eminent People

I met Queen Elizabeth again on more than one occasion, in London and in Delhi, when she was visiting our country. I can't say that we've been in constant touch, but I think she would recognize me, as indeed she had when once we were in London and were called to Buckingham Palace for a garden party.

One thing I must point out about Queen Elizabeth was that on the day of my investiture in Delhi, she had earlier visited Amritsar to pay tribute to the victims of the Jallianwala Bagh massacre. When she entered the room where I was waiting, she was in a rather sombre mood, and I was told that her experience was not entirely as per her expectations. But she quickly changed her mood and asked me what I had done in England. I told her I had played cricket at a very high level, had gone hiking in Scotland, which was her favourite territory, among the many other things I had done. She smiled and said, 'Oh, I can see you've done all the right things. You made good use of your ten years in the UK.' She was a very good conversationalist indeed.

I have met her son, Prince Charles, too on a number of occasions. He is very gracious and charming, and even invited me to his country home in Gloucestershire, where I went with some of my CII friends. We have met often at various functions, and he always picks me out and recognizes me. I've not interacted too closely with his two brothers, Prince Andrew and Prince Edward.

I've already talked about John Major, who was the successor to Margaret Thatcher as the prime minister of England. He held India in high regard, and we continued our relationship well after he laid down the office of prime minister of the UK.

During the year when I was president of the CII, I also had the occasion to meet President Boris Yeltsin of the Soviet Union. I remember in my meeting with him at the CII, there was something he wanted to take up, which was not on the agenda. When I politely pointed this out to him, he brushed me aside. So, naturally, I had to keep quiet and let him have his way with altering the agenda.

In my time as CII president, I also met Chancellor Helmut Kohl of Germany. Our meeting was of the usual kind, very formal, and nothing much emerged from it. But then, after dinner at the Taj Mahal hotel in Delhi, some of us from the team went to the topmost floor for a drink, when in walked the chancellor, unannounced and unaccompanied by anyone. He had been deprived of a drink during dinnertime, and he liked his beer. He came up and joined us in a very friendly manner with a lot of bonhomie. I remember we spent an entertaining one hour at that restaurant and at the Taj in Delhi, recounting our experiences. He was a totally different person after he'd had a glass or two of beer. And surprisingly, he told us that he appreciated Indian beer as much as he did his own German brew!

Another person I remember very well is Mother Teresa. Her Sisters of Charity have a branch in Jamshedpur, and we have helped and supported them for many years. One day, Sisters of Charity told us that they would like to bring Mother Teresa to Jamshedpur. At that time, she was not a saint. I welcomed the visit, and Daisy and I spent a good day meeting her. She attended a function planned by us and also invited us to her Sisters of Charity establishment, where we went. We could make out that she was a genuinely helpful person, totally devoted to the welfare of the downtrodden. I think it is to India's credit that she was given the Bharat Ratna.

I also recall my association and meeting with Naval Tata, Ratan Tata's father. Here, the connection was through my father. Naval Tata was the chairman of the Indian Hockey Federation (IHF) for many years, for almost as long as my father, J.D. Irani, was the treasurer of the IHF. So, the two of them used to meet at IHF events and were on first-name terms with each other. Though I had never really visited Naval Tata in Mumbai, it so happened that one day he came to Jamshedpur to deliver the Michael John Memorial Lecture. Russi Mody was not in town on that day, so it was left to Daisy and me to host him.

We met him at the airport and took him to the director's bungalow. For lunch, he had no company, so we invited him to our home for lunch. He came very willingly. And the surprising thing was that he started talking, almost non-stop, about his family and his other connections. He came for lunch but stayed over till dinnertime. We arranged his dinner also at home. And I think, in total, he must have spent 8–10 hours with us. He told us all the ins and outs of his family, of his break-up, of his first marriage, and his romance and wedding to Simone, who, happily, is still with us. He was a very lovable, friendly, accommodating person and was happy to share his experiences with us.

I would now like to move to the prime ministers of India. My encounter with Indira Gandhi was brief, but it was enough to show me her indomitable spirit and administrative ability. She was invited to Jamshedpur in 1980 by J.R.D. Tata, for Tata Steel's seventy-fifth anniversary. Though JRD had extended an invite to host her in our director's bungalow, she turned it down.

Dr Jagannath Mishra was the chief minister of Bihar then, and he had insisted that she stay in the circuit house. She dined with us at the director's bungalow, however. Jagannath Misra was also there to welcome her. The minute she got out of the car, she turned on him furiously, saying that the circuit house was very dirty.

Apparently, the way her room and the circuit house were decorated was not up to her taste. She felt suffocated in the room that was allotted to her; when she tried to open the window, she couldn't because it was freshly painted and the paint had jammed the window. That annoyed her a lot. Though I was not present at the table, JRD was, and I believe she complained throughout dinner about the poor state of affairs in Bihar, much to the embarrassment of the chief minister.

I have a very high opinion of Narasimha Rao, as the person who saved India's economy. He turned it around in the early 1990s, with the help of people like Manmohan Singh, who was his finance minister, and P. Chidambaram, who was his commerce minister. This was in 1991–92, when India's gold was taken to Geneva and London as security for a loan of $5 billion meant to prop up our economy. Narasimha Rao gave full support to Manmohan Singh to open up the country. I was the president of the CII and so had a ringside view of the action. I personally feel that very little credit is given to Narasimha Rao for his role in dressing up the Indian economy. History must find a much greater place for him in the Indian governance structure than what he has been given up to now.

I accompanied Narasimha Rao on one delegation visit. Mahathir Mohamad was then in his first stint as President of Malaysia. Welcoming us to his office in Kuala Lumpur, he waved a finger at Narasimha Rao. He then said, 'Mr Prime Minister, don't get involved in doing business; leave it to these gentlemen [pointing at us]. They know how to do business. Governments don't. And so, leave the business end of your administration to people from the sector who have been running businesses all their lives. You concentrate on your political ambitions.'

I don't know whether Narsimha Rao took his advice, but there was certainly the opening up of the Indian economy that happened during his time.

Manmohan Singh was quite a stickler for time and protocol. I remember after he became prime minister, I had gone to him for a very minor matter. He had given me time previously. On the same morning, the entire US delegation, with the US ambassador in Delhi, was also waiting for him, regarding the Indo–US nuclear treaty—a path-breaking effort on the part of Manmohan Singh, who forged this alliance. When I entered and saw all those diplomats gathered, I thought, 'Well, that's it. Obviously, I won't get any time or space.' But exactly at the appointed time, his secretary came up to me and said, 'You can have a few minutes with the prime minister.' And all the people in the room, including the US ambassador and his important colleagues from Washington, DC, were made to wait. I went in and met the prime minister, and finished whatever relatively unimportant work I had. The incident showed me the respect the prime minister had for even the smallest of commitments.

One other meeting that I would like to touch upon was with President George Bush, the senior. I had made good friends with the Timken family during my time with the Tatas, as Timken had a joint venture with the Tatas to make bearings in Jamshedpur. When I was in Chicago, I informed Tim Timken—whom I had come to know because of his visits to Jamshedpur—that I was in Chicago and would like to meet him. He immediately gave me a date at an exclusive private club. He said, 'I will not tell you the name of my other guest, but come to this club and we can certainly meet.'

When I went over there I noticed that there was a third chair. He still wouldn't tell me who the third person was, but while we were having drinks, in walked President Bush, who was a very good personal friend of the Timken family. I was a bit taken aback. Tim Timken introduced me as a friend in the industry, and we all had a very enjoyable dinner. Maybe there was security outside the club room where we were meeting, but in the private dining room there was nobody else, just the three of us. It made me think of the type of security we had in India. Our politicians had rows and rows of security officials standing in attendance. Here, it was just Timken, me and the President of the USA. Obviously, they have a very different system of looking after VIPs. That was my only encounter with the US President.

Speaking of eminent people, one person I've left out is Nani Palkhivala. The whole world knows that he was a very eminent jurist, and the whole of India respected him. Though his fame and his impact extended far beyond the Tata house, he was, for many years, a colleague of J.R.D. Tata and the director on the board of Tata Sons, where I was fortunate to get to know him. We often sat next to each other and exchanged pleasantries at Bombay House during lunchtime. When he retired and moved out of his fourth-floor office in Bombay House, I was privileged to occupy that space. Going through the drawers of my desk, I came across several personal papers which he had not bothered to remove, and I passed these on to his family members.

At one time he impacted me directly. It was when we had a problem in the Tata Steel top management. I had occasion to visit him, almost at midnight, at his flat in Colaba. He allowed me in with Ratan Tata, who was accompanying me, and immediately opened his voluminous bookcase. He knew exactly which law the issue pertained to and, within five minutes, had the book open at the relevant paragraphs of the law.

I remember he rebuked me saying, 'You people know how to make steel, and maybe profitably also, but you don't know the first thing about running a company according to law or legal matters.' This was because I had signed something inadvertently which was going to rebound on us. So he, first of all, made sure what the law was and how we had transgressed it. He then told us about the route that was open to us to redress that situation. Obviously, I cannot put on paper all the details. Enough to say that he rebuked me quite comprehensively and deservedly for having jumped the gun and put my signature on a paper which would have landed us all in difficulty. That was my only direct contact with him on legal issues.

What I Tried to Achieve as CEO

I became CEO in 1991, when I was already fifty-five years old. I sat down with my friend and adviser Warren Deverell, whom I come to respect and admire when he helped us in Jamshedpur as a consultant from Arthur D. Little. After Arthur D. Little had completed their work, he stayed back as my personal adviser. And with his advice and help, I wrote down what I must do as CEO.

The first point in my mind was to develop a personal vision. Fortunately for me, my plans were very straightforward. I had no wish to leave Tata Steel and go job-hopping from one corporation to another. So naturally, I saw my future at Tata Steel only. And what did I want to accomplish? I obviously wanted to do as much good as possible for Tata Steel and have the satisfaction of seeing it become a successful, modern and vibrant steel plant. So that was the first item.

The second point was to 'tell the truth about current reality'. I have always been a fanatic with respect to truth; I believe that if one tries to hide the actual facts, life only gets more and more complicated. I remember the saying, 'What a tangled web we weave, when first we practise to deceive.' So, it is a religion with me to be truthful throughout, even though very often it could be inconvenient.

The third point was: do the tough things no one else wants to do. As CEO, I wanted do all the tough things that nobody else in the organization wanted to do, but these tough things had to be done for the betterment of the corporation. Also for the betterment of society. So, I would take the responsibility of becoming unpopular if necessary, and do the difficult things and not pass the buck either to my juniors or to my successors.

The fourth point was: restructure the top team, if necessary. Now, in any organization, there are bound to be different views, but that is fine as long as those views are mutually respected by the participants and they all work together as a team. I'm a supporter of TEAM (Together Everyone Achieves More). So I would restructure the team if required. I believe that most people, if they see a move as reasonable, would follow the rest of the team. But very few humans (maybe less than 1 per cent) would be stubborn and stick to their contrary view, in spite of all the evidence against it. Such people, I feel, should be identified and given the chance to rectify their thinking. But if, after all the efforts, they continue to be obstructive, then one has to remove them—eliminate them from the team. And there are many examples of this I can give from my career. There was a person who could have been an asset to the organization but became an obstructer, and finally we had to part ways with him.

The next item, number five, was building a powerful guiding coalition between the management and the board. Some managing directors (particularly those who nominate themselves as chairman and managing director) feel that they're all powerful and that the board is superfluous. They believe in what is known as the 'mushroom culture'—treat the board as if they are growing mushrooms. (Mushrooms, as you know, grow best in a dark environment, with occasionally some garbage thrown at them.) So in such a culture, the top man feels that he is all important and the board does not matter. I've seen that personally in some organizations. Personally, I very much regarded the board as a guide and as a help to me when I worked as the chief executive. On the Tata Steel board, we had many respected and very important people who had large organizations of their own, like Keshav Mahindra, Nusli Wadia and many others. And they brought a wealth of experience to the board. And I felt it would be stupid of me not to involve them in the management of Tata Steel. I would readily go to them for advice and very often even changed my views if I felt they had a positive contribution to make.

The next point is very important: guide the creation of a shared vision. Everyone in a group, whether it comprises four or 40,000 people, wants to feel that they have contributed to what the company is trying to do: 'shared vision'. And ultimately, if you are a skilful negotiator, you will get your own way, but make it sound and feel as if it is their way. That is the trick.

When I realized that even after eighty years we had no vision statement, I asked all the employees, not just the officers, to give their views. We asked around 400 of them what our vision should be. Some wrote four-page letters on a vision, some just one letter, one word. So we debated that. The debate took us about 2–3 months. And it required a very independent, clear-thinking and unfettered approach. One day I was flying from Jamshedpur to Chennai. We were 40,000 feet above the ground. And I said, 'It's time to now finally put down the vision.' It took me just twenty minutes to write four sentences, which became the vision of Tata Steel. I presented it to the workers, and they all felt there was something that everyone had contributed. I don't have that statement here, but everyone accepted it. The last point of the vision, I remember, was, 'Where Tata Steel aspires to go, others will follow.' And I think that was the clincher.

People felt that they were number one. And because they felt they were number one, they did become number one. This is the power that the CEO has to light. I did not say that I had written that vision. I presented it as their vision. So everyone felt that they had created the vision. Nobody wants to be dictated to or be led by the nose. Even if someone is the lowest person in the hierarchy, he wants to feel that he has contributed something to the company's future. You lose nothing and don't become poorer by giving credit. Please remember, as you go higher in the hierarchy, give credit where credit is due, not falsely.

Be honest in giving credit to others for free. Don't say this or that is your idea. Make them feel that it is their idea, and then they will respond. And the power of compounding the thoughts of 40,000 people against one person's thought is tremendous. Everyone then strives to become number one. Yes, you put the target before them. Obviously, it involves change, and you then become the main agent for that change.

This is one thing which I am very proud to share. We had (we still have) a system whereby executives could change cars every three years if they were senior and every six years if they were junior. I inherited a car, a good one from my predecessor, and I used the same one for fifteen years. I did not change it. It was perfectly fine. The company's garage was there to look after it. Finally, they told me that they had changed everything in the car, except the shell. But it was the same car, same registration, same colour, same shape. And that was to make people feel: Look, if you don't need it, why spend on it? Once they see the chief executive doing this, many people feel inspired and wish to emulate him.

So take the responsibility of being the main agent of change. Don't leave it for the next fellow. Don't have the attitude that goes: well, it's okay for everybody, but not for me, I am the chief executive. Since you are the chief executive, you have to implement the change first. Have you ever known, or have you ever felt comfortable going to, a doctor who smokes a lot or drinks a lot, is obese, has high blood pressure? Would you ask such a doctor to give you a prescription for good health? Even if they gave you a prescription, you would not follow it. So you have to live the way you want others to live. This is very important for chief executives.

The next point on my agenda was to create endless opportunities for two-way communication. During my time as chief executive, which ended in 2001, the mobile phone had just come into the market, but there was no Internet or email. So, to communicate, I had to go physically, and I still feel that is the best way to communicate. When you look at the person straight in the eye or give him a warm handshake, the message that you convey has a far better effect than when someone looks at it as an email or an SMS.

Though Tata Steel was spread out over a vast area, I would utilize at least fifty half-days per year to go and speak to what are known as Joint Departmental Councils (JDC) at TISCO. There are about fifty of them, and I would spend one half-day with each, just listen to the people along with the union bosses. And they would not say anything revolutionary. Sometimes a brilliant thing would come up. But mostly it was grumbles, such as my grade is not good or my house roof is leaking and things like that. But you have to listen to them and give them the assurance that it if it is so today, tomorrow you will find it a bit different.

I will give you one example. Someone once told me, 'What you are trying to do to reduce the numbers of people, taking away jobs, all that is fine. But the roof of my house is leaking badly.'

So I asked the housing department to carry out a survey, and they found that around 7000 houses had not been repaired, including, by the way, my own (one part of my house was leaking). I asked how much it would cost to carry out the repairs. The figure was some crores, and in the usual course of things, we would have taken several years to reach that figure, as it could not have gone through the normal maintenance budget. And by the time we would have finished, more repair requests would be in the pipeline.

So I sanctioned several crores of rupees on a one-time basis and said to those people, 'Look, in one year you employ whoever you want. But in one year, all those complaints about leaking roofs should go.' And we did it!

People understood that once we put our minds to something we could solve any problem. Cost has never been an issue when it comes to bringing about improvements. It is the mind. It is the mindset more than the mind. I have found that money is never a constraint. Creativity, thinking, those are the constraints. So once you can think a problem through, you will always be able to succeed.

Another problem is communication. I have written two-way communication and not one-way communication. With two-way communication, we allow people to express their views. I used to have meetings with my officers, 2000 people at a big auditorium, and everyone was free to say what they wanted. They could complain against their boss but under one condition—if they made a frivolous, incorrect complaint, which I would find out after my investigation, I would fire them publicly in the next meeting. Because they made complaints publicly, the boss was made to look small in front of 2000 people. So I, in turn, would come back the next time and say to them, 'What you told me was not true. You lied.' And make that man feel small, once again in front of the same 2000 people. So that cut out the frivolity from their complaints.

The next point is something which we have now taken as a religion, to create opportunities for innovations among the rank and file. We appointed a consultant at the start of our rejuvenation exercise. They would go to all the departments, talk to the junior people and senior people, and come up with ideas for innovation and improvements. Then, they would go and discuss those ideas with their bosses, and the bosses would usually say, 'Oh, I tried this thing out fifteen years ago. It didn't work.' When I told them to put the ideas down as suggestions regardless, the consultants went through implementing these suggestions for over six months. We created a mechanism to do that. And we came up with a set of improvements, which, in fact, helped us to become the lowest-cost producer of steel in the world.

Human ingenuity doesn't come only from the bosses. It comes equally from people lower down the hierarchy. I had a practice as chief executive: whenever somebody did something exceptional I would reward them on the spot.

I remember this one night when one of our largest blast furnaces had stopped charging on its own. A blast furnace has to be fed from the bottom through what is known as a skip. The skip that went up and fed the material into that particular furnace had stopped working. And for the next two days, all the top engineers of blast furnaces attempted to rectify the problem, but they couldn't succeed. There was a gentleman associated with blast furnaces whom we wanted to contact. But he had taken the weekend off. Finally, on Monday morning, he returned. He went behind the panels of electronic instruments and did something which we did not know, and things started working again. Everyone clapped, hugged him, shook his hands. And I just said to him, 'Come to my office at eleven o'clock.'

So he came to my office at eleven, looking very smug, aware of my reputation as someone who rewarded people on the spot, expecting a big reward. But I fired him. I fired him for not sharing his knowledge with others, because we could only succeed as a team. In this case, he did not show that team spirit. I fired him and, in a few weeks, he left the organization. We don't want individualists. The days of Isaac Newton and people like him are gone. We have to succeed as a team.

Finally, the most important point, which I believe is credibility. A chief executive or even a prime minister cannot achieve anything on his own unless he has the support of his team, which may be five people or 5000 or 5 million. How does he get the support of the team? By building credibility. When he's talking to people, they must think, 'Yes, he's saying something which he believes in. And tomorrow, he will do something about what he's saying today.' So that is credibility. It will take years to establish it. And it can go in the blink of an eye.

The credibility of the Tatas means that we will not do anything dishonest, whatever be the consequences. If I am asked what is one feature that a leader or managing director or CEO must have, my answer will be: of course, he must be clever; he must know his subject; he must be humane and all that. But credibility is the key attribute. Without credibility, people will not follow him.

Lastly, my aim was to preserve the core values of the Tatas and my own.

The one very important thing which I think any CEO must do from the first day onwards is to identify and start training his successor. When I became the CEO, Mr Tata, the senior, called me and said, 'I want you to always keep two names in your pocket or in your wallet, two names. You may change them, but you must have them at any time. One, of someone whom you see as worthy of your position five or ten years down the line and whom you will train. And the second name should be of someone who is going to lead the organization if, by chance, by misfortune, you step out of this building today and you are hit by a bus and go upstairs who is going to lead the organization? You can keep on changing them as often as you want, but these are must-haves for the benefit of the organization.'

I'm totally against those organizations where they form search committees, which keep getting three-year extensions. That sort of CEO, in my opinion, is not serving the company.

I read this in a newspaper. Imagine you have a bucket of water. If you want to measure how your organization will miss you when you leave, put your hand into the water, splash it around, swish it, create waves, bubbles, and then withdraw your hand. The impression left in the water after you pull out your hand is the measure by which your organization will miss you on your departure.

Aspects I Did Well In

1. I think I have done a reasonably good job in enforcing the Tata values. I did not allow unfair practices at Tata Steel and tried to weed out any person or practice that was not in line with the principles the Tatas stood for.
2. I have been instrumental—supported, of course, by the commitment of my team—in taking Tata Steel to the pinnacle of the steel world. Under my leadership, various aspects of the company's working have been modernized, and maintaining the highest quality remains a priority. I also took the initiative to build bridges in the international steel community, particularly with the British.
3. I held myself to the highest moral standards regarding fairness in my day-to-day dealings with all concerned. I never did any personal favour to family or friends, and fostered honesty in business dealings as well as in human relationships.
4. My greatest satisfaction has been that I've taught my three children the correct values in life.

Certain Aspects Where I Could Have Done Better

1. I could not take Tata Steel beyond Indian shores and establish production units in other countries. I also did not succeed in establishing production plants for Tata Steel outside Jamshedpur. We remained a one-location steel plant throughout my leadership.
2. I could have managed the very important aspect of succession in a more business-like and efficient manner.
3. I neglected the role of women in our organization and could have done more in this regard.
4. Though it is always acknowledged that it is lonely at the top, I might have paid more attention to not being such a loner! I lacked warmth in my communication and many have told me that I was looked upon with respect, but it was not necessary to be looked upon with awe. Daisy played a vital role in softening my persona. I became more approachable because of her warmth and friendly behaviour.

Epilogue

Zubin Irani

Dad was a father, a mentor and a friend to the family. My sisters, Niloufer and Tanaaz, and I spent our formative years in Jamshedpur, going to school there until our 10th/12th grades, and for many of those years (1980–2000) he was the president/ managing director of Tata Steel. Many people ask me if it was hard growing up under his vast shadow, as his son. Frankly, it was not hard at all; it was, in fact, a privilege being his son.

Devoted Family Man

Most in Jamshedpur saw Dad as a 'tough and decisive leader', but few knew that he was also a very devoted family man. In the 1980s and '90s, despite his hectic schedule, he always found the time to have dinner with the family from 8 p.m. to 9 p.m., following which he and my mother, Daisy, would go out for their daily social commitments. And very often they would return by 10.30 p.m. and take the family on a drive through the town of Jamshedpur. It was his way of assessing the progress that was being made in the plant/town and, at the same time, bonding with the family. For

Dad, his family and kids were his Achilles' heel. I remember the time he gave up eating meat and eggs for one year, when my sister Tanaaz fell seriously ill. Dad also never forgot those instances where any of his kids came in 'harm's way' or had 'near misses', and always claimed that those were the most difficult moments of his life—and he remembered and recounted those incidents till the very end of his life.

On one of our trips to the US, our host was reversing his car at a high speed and almost backed into my younger sister Tanaaz. He remembered that day vividly and would keep bringing it up in conversation even two decades later.

He would insist that we as a family go on a vacation for 7–10 days every year and organized the trips himself every year over the past thirty years. All we needed to do as kids was to show up with our families. It was his way of keeping the family together and closely bonded. There was a decade when he was into cruises, and we must have gone on every cruise in the world. Thank God that phase eventually wore off. Dad would also take the family along for short weekend trips (when we were in school in Jamshedpur) to Noamundi (iron ore mines), West Bokaro (coal mines), Jamadoba, etc. During these trips, I remember he would try and spend time with his officers/teams but also bond with the family.

While he loved all his children, he was clearly closest to my sister Tanaaz, who was the youngest and, as a result, had spent the most time with him at home. She could get away with anything, and he would simply accept her point of view. He was very proud of my sister Niloufer and thought of her as a very selfless person, very often calling her Florence Nightingale. Given that I had spent many years abroad in the US and Singapore, he was closer to my sisters, who lived in Mumbai and got to see him much more often. I remember vividly that he got most upset or sad when he saw us arguing or fighting with each other. One of the few instances when he hit me was when I pushed my sister in anger, and she fell and broke her arm. It was a moment I will never forget, and his actions then sent a very clear message to me on how to treat my sisters moving forward.

Relationship between Mom and Dad

Dad met Mom in 1970, when he had moved to Jamshedpur to work at Tata Steel. Mom's father was an officer in the company, and she was born and grew up in the town. They fell in love and got married in 1971. While they shared common values, they were also very different personalities. Mom was much more social and friendly, and I recall that when we had larger official parties at our home, she was an amazing hostess, working her way through the crowd and making everyone feel at home. Dad, on the other hand, was much more reserved, and one would typically find him at one table, talking to a few people that he knew well and felt comfortable with. He was never someone who worked the room or enjoyed small talk.

Mom showed a tremendous passion for serving the community and took on many roles with local organizations. She was overall a great complement and support to Dad, and he always acknowledged that to us. One thing I learnt from both is never to go to bed without making up with your spouse (if you've had a fight). This was a rule that Dad followed, and he mentioned that to me and Priya when we got married. It has helped our relationship tremendously over the years.

Values

From my very early years, I remember him instilling a deep sense of work ethic in my sisters and me, mainly by being the role model. He worked long hours, including full Saturdays and even Sunday mornings (when he would take me along with him to his office, and I would do my homework). The phrase that I remember him using many times was, 'Luck is when preparation meets with opportunity.'

Whenever I took my exams in high school, he always said the only thing I could do was to be fully prepared and give it my best. Then leave the rest to God. That is all he asked of me and my sisters in everything we did. As a child, I got to spend many weekends travelling with him to various places in India and got a great sense of the work ethic and dedication he brough to his job, and this influenced me a lot.

Dad and Mom both ensured that my sisters and I grew up grounded in humility, despite the rather privileged lives we led in Jamshedpur, being their children, in a town where the inhabitants were either employees of Tata companies or suppliers to them. The few times I recall getting spanked by him were instances where I had treated anyone with disrespect or hurt them. One instance will always stay with me. When I was around ten years old I shouted and behaved rudely with a local instructor/caddy on a golf course and bragged about it to my sisters. When he found out about it, not only did he give me a real walloping, but he also went with me to apologize to the individual, and that left a clear impression on me, that I had to treat everyone with dignity and respect, irrespective of their background and social standing.

Growing up in Jamshedpur, we had many people working in our household, and not even once did he raise his voice with any of them. Dad also ensured that my sisters and I always integrated with the larger community in Jamshedpur and never considered ourselves privileged in any way. And I suspect that was why he insisted that we go to school in Jamshedpur until

our 12th grade, and why he encouraged me to go to engineering
school (IIT) in India.

He taught me to always speak my mind and do the tough
things that nobody wanted to do. One day in 1991, when I was
studying in Delhi, I visited him in his suite at the Taj Palace. I
was very surprised to meet his PA from Jamshedpur, Krishna
Rao. I asked him why he had brought Mr Rao along. He sat me
down one on one and explained to me that he felt he had been
treated wrongly by Russi Mody (then Tata Steel MD); so he was
drafting a letter to Mr Mody and the Tata Steel board voicing
his discontent. The only person he trusted to draft that letter was
Krishna Rao, and that was why he had brought him with him to
Delhi. He explained to me that there was a risk that he might lose
his job at the company if the board did not back him, but he felt
it was the right thing for him to do, irrespective of anything else.
I personally saw many more instances where he took very difficult
calls that ultimately benefited the company in its transformation.
Interestingly, towards the end of his stint at Tata Steel, he did
mend his relationship with Russi Mody, and I think that brough
him a lot of joy and satisfaction. Another lesson there was never to
hold a grudge and be willing to forgive/mend relationships.

Perhaps the biggest value and attribute that we all, as children,
learnt from him was maintaining 'credibility'. I remember his
telling me many times that I would always have my credibility
until I lose it the first time. And if I lose it once, it will be lost
forever. He role-modelled this behaviour in everything he did. I
remember one dinner-table conversation where he told us about a
supplier to Tata Steel who had offered him a '3 per cent cut' of the
total order value. Which, apparently, was done with many other
companies in India at that time. He told us that his immediate
response to the supplier was to reduce the price by 3 per cent, and
then he signed the contract. I also recall another classic. I did my

11th and 12th classes at a boarding school in the Delhi region. During my interview process (where my father accompanied me), the principal asked Dad what the Tatas could donate towards a new swimming pool that was being built. My father's response was immediate and spontaneous: 'A bucket of water.' He was very clear with the principal in front of me that I would have to be chosen on my own merit and that his company would not be able to donate anything. Interestingly, I still got admitted. In fact, two days before he passed away in an ICU, he told me that he had never intentionally lied to anyone or done anything unethical, and that was perhaps what he was most proud of in his life.

While Dad always had aspirations for me, he never imposed his views in terms of where I should study, what I should study and where I should work. While I always consulted him on these important decisions in my life, and he would help provide a framework to evaluate the various options, even help make connections, ultimately, he let me make my own decisions and chart my own path. He then backed and supported me 100 per cent on my decisions, with no regrets. When I moved from a general management/P&L role to private equity, I could tell that he was not completely comfortable. Partly because he did not completely understand the private equity industry. He, however, embraced my decision and backed me once I had made the move. His love and support towards his family was clearly unconditional. This has been a big learning for Priya and me as we help guide our two boys in their decisions. He clearly wanted me to chart my own journey and lead my own life.

Relationship with His Father, Jiji Irani

In many respects, Dad's very strong relationship with his father, Jiji, helped shape our strong bond. While Jiji died when I was only one year old, I know that Dad shared a very strong bond with him. Jiji was like a friend to him and was very involved in his upbringing. He encouraged Dad to go to college in England and then come back to India to work for the Tatas. Jiji was also a very good-hearted, well-liked and well-respected man in the Parsi community in India. I could tell that their bond was extremely strong, and he missed Jiji for decades after his passing. Every time the topic of his father would come up, Dad would have tears in his eyes. He was very dedicated to supporting the annual Parsi cricket tournament in Jiji's name, as cricket was a common passion that both shared (and it passed down to me). One regret that Dad always had was that Jiji was not around to witness the success that he enjoyed in his professional career with the Tatas—he died in 1973.

Vision

In the last decade, I have had many discussions with Dad on the life he led, including for that one month prior to his passing, on 31 October 2022 (while he was in the ICU). What emerged very clearly through these discussions was that he was a man with a clear vision. In fact, his vision for Tata Steel to become the lowest-cost producer of steel in the world started in the early 1980s, when he became the GM of the company.

The man he credited the most for his success was J.R.D. Tata. JRD inspired him, challenged him and helped him shape the vision for the company. He also provided him with a lot of support and clearly had his back. I can distinctly remember how sad Dad was when JRD passed away in November 1993. He flew to Europe for his funeral.

His vision for Tata Steel began to take shape almost a decade before he took over as the CEO, in 1991. Timing also played a big role. India liberalized and opened up to competition in 1991, which helped build a strong case for the transformation of Tata Steel into the lowest-cost producer of steel in the world.

Leadership

Dad was a coach and mentor to me throughout my career. Perhaps the best advice he gave me was when I transitioned from being an associate partner at McKinsey to becoming MD for Carrier India in 2006. Coming from McKinsey, I was determined to develop a 'winning strategy for the business', and I remember his telling me that strategy was 20 per cent of the solution. Eighty per cent was execution, and that had to do with building the right team, aligning and incentivizing the organization appropriately, and constantly guiding them, often managing conflict. He told me that a CEO role was all about working with 'people' and required a lot of patience at times. It was a rude awakening for me, but he was 100 per cent correct. He was a tremendous support to me during that period.

There are many lessons in leadership that I have learnt from Dad:

1) He would often tell me that **building followership and strong relationships** is the most important leadership attribute. Two examples of this stand out distinctly. The first was the very strong relationship he had developed with V.G. Gopal, Tata Steel's union leader, who was unfortunately assassinated in 1993. I recall how, when I was a child, he would insist that I accompany him every year for V.G. Gopal's birthday to his home. And I remember how happy Gopal would be when he saw me with Dad. He would feed me and play with me. Now when I think about it, this was a terrific way to build stronger

relationships. Another technique he used very effectively was to send personal 'yellow' notes to officers in the company, whenever they did something well or sometimes even with constructive criticism or suggestions. I have met numerous officers who have shown me these notes, and I could tell how much it mattered to them that he cared so much. Long after he stepped down as the CEO of Tata Steel, he maintained a very close relationship with his office staff and people he had worked closely with, always being available and helping them through their journey. Many of them travelled often to Jamshedpur over the past decade to spend time with him, and I saw the joy and excitement in his eyes when he met them. My sense, having watched many of the interactions closely, is that he always had their best interests in mind and always had their back as well. They knew that whatever he told them (pleasant or not) was keeping their best interests in mind. This was repeated and confirmed to me by several of his ex-team members after his passing.

2) Dad **was very objective and fair** with his team. Above all, he let his performance do the talking and always thought about the company first. I did notice that he formed strong relationships with select people in the company, and those people were loyal to him; however, he never let his friendships drive his decision-making. He always tried to promote the best man/woman for the job and, in fact, shared several examples with me where he had passed over people he knew well because he did not believe they were the best candidates for the job. This was the case with his own succession in the company as well.

3) Finally, I learnt a lot from how he **incentivized people in his team and organization to perform**. My favourite example here is when he was embarking on the company transformation,

he knew that the officers and workers would be working very hard. He also knew that they would need the support of their spouses. So he arranged for the spouses to visit the factory and started a monthly dialogue with the spouse community. His belief was that this would make them more aware of the challenges the company was facing and the severe conditions the employees were working under. He told me that this helped build a lot more support from the household, which made the employees more productive in their jobs.

Priya

The best advice that Dad gave me was on my most important decision—choosing my life partner, Priya. Priya's father worked at Tata Steel, and we have been childhood friends since our school days in Jamshedpur. In fact, Priya was my sister Niloufer's best friend. Dad had watched her growing up for many years and was extremely fond of her. We dated during our later school and college years but eventually drifted apart. In fact, in all honesty, she broke the relationship, and I had been deeply hurt. One day, on a visit to the US in 1998, where I was pursuing my postgraduate degree in engineering, he asked me about Priya and whether I had been in touch with her. I told him that I was done with the relationship and would never go down that path again. He sensed pain in my voice and told me that I should never let my 'ego come in the way' and that if the opportunity presented itself again I should give it another sincere try, because Priya was special. I was surprised at that time to hear those words from him, but reflected on them and eventually saw the wisdom in them. As it turns out, Priya and I reconnected around six months later by accident, and I followed Dad's advice. We were married in April 2000 and have been happily married now for twenty-three years.

Over the years, I saw that Dad and Priya's relationship was very special; they were very close. He said that she was his third daughter and fourth child. Dad was also very close to his two sons-in-law, Yezdi and Cyrus, who are an integral part of our family. And while he had five grandsons, Dad's one regret was that he never had a granddaughter.

Conclusion

I did not have the opportunity to work closely with Dad professionally, but I can tell you that he was a great leader at home—a role he played very well until the day he passed away. While many others saw him as a strong leader in the corporate world, our family was extremely fortunate to see the human side of him, as an endearing father and devoted husband. He was a great coach and role model to me as well as to my sisters. He will be remembered very fondly for the life he led and for the lives he touched along the way.

Scan QR code to access the
Penguin Random House India website